HIDDEN GARDENS

HIDDEN
GARDENS

Foreword by Chris Beardshaw

Penny David

Cassell Illustrated

To my Mother
and all the Hidden Gardeners

This book is published to accompany the television series entitled
Hidden Gardens, which was first broadcast in 2002. The series was
produced by BBC Wales.

Series producers: John Trefor and Lynda Maher
Executive producer: Christina Macaulay
Production manager: Catrin Parry

First published in Great Britain in 2002 by Cassell Illustrated,
a division of Octopus Publishing Group Limited
2-4 Heron Quays, London E14 4JP

By arrangement with the BBC
The BBC logo is a registered trademark of the
British Broadcasting Corporation and is used under licence.

BBC logo © BBC 1996
Hidden Gardens © BBC 2002
Copyright © 2002 Octopus Publishing Group Limited

Text © 2002 Penny David
Photographs © 2002 Rowan Isaac, apart from those
specified in the picture credits on page 175.

A CIP catalogue record for this book is available from the British Library.

1 2 3 4 5 6 7 8 9 10

ISBN 0 304 36442 8

Consultant editor: Pippa Rubinstein
Project editor: Patricia Burgess
Designer: Judith Robertson
Additional picture research: Robin Douglas-Withers
Indexer: Margaret Cornell

Printed in Italy

Contents

Lyveden New Bield   10

Restoration has uncovered a garden frozen in time, unfinished since the owner's death in 1605, with an exquisite garden lodge flanked by moats and 'snail' mounts. Imprisoned for his religious beliefs by Elizabeth I, Sir Thomas Tresham described his plans in fine detail (and almost unintelligible handwriting) to his gardener. Today one task is to decipher his instructions and to seek out the symbolism underlying his message.

Aberglasney   38

Once described as 'lost in time', these gardens became famous when a television series featured their rescue from dereliction. Bishop Rudd's Cloister Garden (a unique survival from around 1600) put Aberglasney firmly on the historic gardens map. Yet this is the last part of it to be restored. Archaeology has come up with clues, but no plans survive. How will the restoration team decide on its design?

St Fagans   67

A cluster of Victorian and Edwardian layouts provide the setting for the fine Jacobean 'castle' at the core of what is now the Museum of Welsh Life. Recent attention has focused on the wider landscape, but now the formal gardens adjacent to the house are being restored. Their turn-of-the-century muse was Gay Paget, a member of the society sect known as the Souls. Research in the archives helps restorers to re-create her Italian Garden.

Lawrence Johnston's property was the first to be taken on by the National Trust simply for its garden's sake. Now it is one of Britain's most visited gardens, and its innovative hedged 'rooms' are legendary. Fifty years on, as areas of the garden call for refurbishment, a renewed impulse to get closer to Johnston's original planting schemes poses tantalizing questions, not least, 'What was actually planted here?' Detective work takes us all over the world in search of the answers.

The architect of Harlow New Town made his own garden near by. Partly a setting for sculpture, partly a place for the planner to play, Sir Frederick Gibberd's layout is acclaimed as one of the great late 20th-century gardens. Trustees face the challenge of maintaining the garden in the spirit of its creator.

Hidden beneath a jungle of burrs, brambles and knotweed lie the bones of a fine Victorian garden clinging to a steep, south-facing slope in remote west Wales. A team of local people are hacking through the undergrowth with a mission to make the garden grow again. How will they fare?

Foreword

Britain has long been recognized as the home of great gardens, but ask a bunch of gardeners what constitutes a great garden and opinions will be divided. From design and structure to plant combinations, atmosphere and technology, the debate rumbles on.

For me, however, more important than all these qualities is a generous helping of passion. Once present, it seems that all the other design ingredients will naturally follow.

Passion from within a gardener is raw and unadulterated. The process of creating a garden is like baring your very soul; it becomes a snapshot of character, encapsulating the personality, thoughts and emotion at the time of the garden's creation.

For this reason alone, it is enlightening to rediscover and revisit the gardens of the past, not only to appreciate the design and horticulture of the day, but also to reawaken the personality of their creator. A garden is nothing without personality.

Chris Beardshaw

June 2002

LYVEDEN NEW BIELD
The Cryptic Coding of Sir Thomas Tresham

Interruptions in garden-making, as in house-building, are not uncommon. Your workmen defect to another site, bad weather delays the job, finances run short. But a gap of some 400 years between listing the plants you want for your orchard and seeing them bear fruit is an unusually long one. This is the time-scale at Lyveden New Bield.

The first sight of the New Bield is quite extraordinary. It is best caught in silhouette against a low sun. A lacy cardboard cut-out perches on a broad, sweeping skyline, as much window as wall. It is no less astonishing on closer approach. You find the finely wrought shell of an elegant classical building frozen in suspended animation. It sits on a grassy eminence, its only close companion a handsome oak two centuries its junior a couple of hundred yards away.

This is hardly hidden, someone whispers; and does it really qualify as a garden? The answer is that there are many ways of being hidden, and that this is indeed a garden, a once and future garden. The Bield was intended to be a garden building – a lodge. It is, admittedly, oddly estranged from its garden setting. It's set at a dog-leg angle beyond the main rectangle of gardens running up the hill, a knight's-move from the symmetry of the water garden complex and its earthworks – features that have always been upstaged by architecture, and are only now beginning to get the attention and understanding they deserve. On the other hand, as we shall see, the Bield was not intended by its maker to stand quite so starkly on its green platform like a model on a table.

The New Bield looks quite new – the stone mullions and ashlar work are as clean and clear cut as on the day the masons put down their chisels – but it is unfinished. The windows are scored for glazing and drilled for window bars, its walls channelled to receive water down-pipes, its main entrance suspended above the ground, waiting for a flight of steps. The original plumbers, glaziers, carpenters and tilers could arrive tomorrow via a time machine to get on with the job.

Rather than noticing such functional details as grooves gouged for window panes, most visitors' eyes will light on the equally crisp

An Outline of the Plot...

Lyveden New Bield was acquired by the National Trust as long ago as 1922 for its outstanding architecture – a fine example of a late 16th-century garden lodge on the skyline of the sweeping Rockingham Forest countryside in Northamptonshire.

One of several idiosyncratic buildings built by wealthy landowner Sir Thomas Tresham, the New Bield expresses Tresham's knowledge of classical architecture and his religious faith, the steadfastness of which brought him persecution and financial hardship.

The lodge became known as the 'new bield' (building) – to distinguish it from the main Manor House (Old Bield) farther down the hill. (Like most houses this old, it has been much altered over the years; it is now in private ownership.) The two buildings were to be connected by an ambitious range of garden features – raised terraces and mounds linked by sizeable canals, and with orchards and parterres. All were typical of the great gardens of the period, of which none now remains intact.

The New Bield was never finished. Why did building stop? How much of the garden was actually completed? It remained in suspended animation through most of the 20th century, but some of these questions are now being answered by persistent research and determined work on the ground.

Recently the National Trust has taken some of the neighbouring farmland into long-term tenancy to secure the garden's boundaries. Clearance of scrub has enhanced the significance of the garden layout and the relationship between the New Bield and its garden, and a restrained planting programme is in process to fulfil Tresham's orchard plans.

The garden has Grade II* status in the English Heritage Register of Historic Parks and Gardens of Special Historic Interest.

A corner of the moat with the bridge.

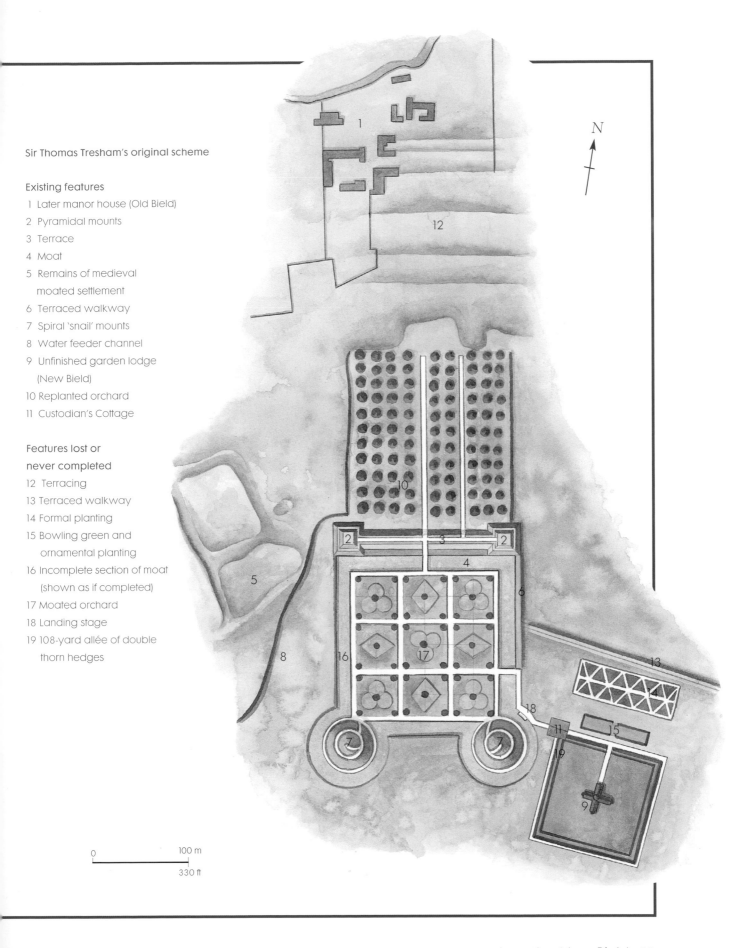

Sir Thomas Tresham's original scheme

Existing features

1 Later manor house (Old Bield)
2 Pyramidal mounts
3 Terrace
4 Moat
5 Remains of medieval
   moated settlement
6 Terraced walkway
7 Spiral 'snail' mounts
8 Water feeder channel
9 Unfinished garden lodge
   (New Bield)
10 Replanted orchard
11 Custodian's Cottage

**Features lost or
never completed**

12 Terracing
13 Terraced walkway
14 Formal planting
15 Bowling green and
   ornamental planting
16 Incomplete section of moat
   (shown as if completed)
17 Moated orchard
18 Landing stage
19 108-yard allée of double
   thorn hedges

N

0   100 m

330 ft

1   2   3   4

The circular metopes carved on the ground-floor frieze represent the seven emblems of the Passion:

1 Symbols combine to form 'IHS', the first three letters of *Ihsus*, the Greek for 'Jesus'.

2 The sacred monogram XP, the first two letters of the Greek word for 'Christ'.

3 Judas's moneybag surrounded by 30 pieces of silver.

4 Weapons, torches of faith and a lantern surrounded by a twisted cord.

5 Scourge, pillar with crown of thorns, and sceptre of reeds. Surround of twisted linen.

6 Ladder, cross with crown of thorns, sponge and spear. Surround is crown of thorns.

7 The seamless garment of Jesus between three dice.

figurative decorations claiming attention on each complex façade. The most detailed is the frieze of circular emblems, known as metopes, in the classical entablature Robert Stickells designed above the ground-floor windows. Some of these finely detailed reliefs are quite arcane, but even in our secular age we might recognize here the Cross and there the sacred monogram XP, and appreciate that these were symbols of some significance to the maker – evidently a religious man.

5   6   7

This is the tip of an iceberg of significance. You can enjoy the place without exploring the maker's intentions further, but to do so is to learn only part of the story. You might as well go to the opera wearing earplugs. It is like visiting some of the great 18th-century landscapes, such as Stowe or Stourhead: you can take visual pleasure in the views of trees, grass and water with incidental buildings as focal points, but this is to skim the surface of an experience. To the original garden-makers these scenes were fraught with classical symbolism and imbued with allusion. Your tour of the garden was carefully planned from point to point, from temple to temple, to guide you through a landscape of allegory and personal meaning. We have an equivalent hidden agenda here. To visit Lyveden without finding out who its maker was and what message he meant his building to convey is to miss out on a cracking good story.

Sir Thomas Tresham made his whole building signify his Christian beliefs. The frieze above the ground-floor windows involves a series of metopes showing emblems of the Passion repeated in various sequences (see opposite). Above them inscriptions in Latin praise Christ, the Virgin and the Cross. The blank heraldic shields at basement level were intended to be carved with symbols embodying Tresham's more personal family and social pride.

Sir Thomas Tresham (1543–1605) painted in 1568. His armour and gun are chased and inlaid with designs of trefoils, the Tresham emblem, and the blackwork embroidery on his collar and wrist ruffles displays the same motif.

Undoubting Thomas

The year after Elizabeth I came to the throne of England in 1558, Thomas Tresham came into his own sizeable inheritance. Aged 15, he became head of a highly upwardly mobile family of minor Northamptonshire gentry. He inherited one of the largest estates in the county from his grandfather, a Catholic who had held office under the Protestant Henry VIII and Edward VI, as well as the Catholic Mary Tudor. His main residences were at Rushton Hall near the market town of Rothwell, and at Lyveden.

Thomas was educated at Christ Church, Oxford, and admitted to the Middle Temple, London, in 1560. Intelligent, cultured, wealthy and well connected, he moved in the highest social circles. He was acquainted with William Cecil, Lord Burghley, creator of 'the most important Elizabethan garden' at Theobalds (pronounced 'tibbalds') Park, Hertfordshire, in the decade 1575–85. Nothing but descriptions of this now remain. He knew Sir Christopher Hatton of Holdenby House and Kirby Hall, in Northamptonshire – both places where innovative gardens were being made. He was knighted at Kenilworth in 1575, at the same time as Robert Cecil, future Earl of Salisbury and builder of Hatfield. It was at Kenilworth in 1575 that Robert Dudley, Earl of Leicester, entertained Elizabeth and her court with waterborne festivities. In 'The Princely Pleasuress of Kenilworth' the castle moat was invaded by tritons, nymphs and dolphins enacting the rescue of the Lady of the Lake through an intervention of the Virgin Queen. Extensive water features began to be a *sine qua non* of the best gardens.

Tresham was evidently bitten by the water-garden bug, as Lyveden shows. But why did he not wield more courtly influence? Why were the Tresham family finances brought to their knees? In fact, they never recovered: the Tresham line died out in the 17th century, though descendants continued to make history. From his daughter

One of Lyveden's two 'snail' mounts. The spiralling path to the summit provides a gradual ascent to a viewing platform, but might also evoke in the Elizabethan mind some notion of the circuitous route to heaven.

Mary's marriage to Thomas Brudenell of Deene was descended the 7th Earl of Cardigan, of Light Brigade and knitted jacket fame.

Part of the answer is that his efficiency in managing his estates and farming progressively was not matched by equally ruthless management of his family and personal affairs. He led an extravagant lifestyle, building ambitiously and entertaining lavishly, as seemed to befit his position. In about 1566 he married Meriel, daughter of Sir Robert Throckmorton. They had 10 children. Four of his six daughters married peers or future peers, and he gave all of them generous marriage portions that perhaps he could not afford. (He even lost out through a niece, his ward, who secretly married a servant. She brought a lawsuit against him for withholding her marriage portion, and he went to the Tower until he paid.) His son and heir caused no end of grief before meeting a sticky end alongside Guy Fawkes in the plot instigated by his neighbour and relative Robert Catesby.

However, what lay at the root of the trouble was Tresham's religion. When, in 1581, the Jesuits sent missionary priests to England to fan the flames of the Catholic faith, Tresham was one of those whose ardour was fired. Some Catholics kept a low profile and outwardly conformed to the Anglican creed. Tresham, however, although he remained loyal to Queen Elizabeth, was among the recusants who refused to put in the required appearance at his parish church. For this he paid dearly. Between 1581 and 1598 he spent lengthy periods in prison or under house arrest. He was also fined heavily as a recusant – some £8000 in total. But more importantly for someone of his ambition, he was disqualified from state office, which meant that he enjoyed none of the influence and perquisites that would have oiled the wheels of his fortune.

All this helps to explain why the New Bield was never finished. And why its design is as exquisitely complicated as it is.

Its cruciform shape modelled by low winter light, the New Bield remains unfinished. It is thought that Sir Thomas planned a third storey (see page 21), which would have made it a far more elaborate and ambitious building. He also intended to surround it with a hedged enclosure. The custodian's cottage on the right was probably built in the late 17th century with stone intended for the lodge.

An A to Z of garden buildings will include names such as banqueting house, belvedere, eyecatcher, gazebo, gloriette, kiosk, pavilion, summer-house, temple… and lodge. The hunting lodge has an ancient pedigree. Garden lodges have always given builders a pretext to be playful – think of all those Victorian lodges marking the entrances to estates where architects could practise on whimsical designs not serious enough for the main house.

Elaborate garden lodges were an established 16th-century tradition. Tresham had already built one at Rushton. 'My other lodge is triangular,' he might have said. Its plan symbolized the Trinity. But the Rushton lodge was functional as well as meaningful: it was built for the warrener, and Sir Thomas made a tidy income from the rabbits raised in the 300-acre warren and sold to poulterers in London as meat and for the skins. (He also had to compensate the neighbours for the depredations of the rabbits.) Sir Thomas was a hard-nosed improving landlord. He built up a great sheep farm by enclosing land ruthlessly. He sold horses, cattle and hogs, plus corn, hops, cheeses, pigeons, hides, timber and lime, as well as all those rabbits burrowing beneath the Rushton lodge.

The cross-shaped lodge at Lyveden was intended as a banqueting house. It houses all the necessary chambers and services of a miniature mansion. The building's three levels include a kitchen, buttery and larder in the basement, a hall and parlour on the raised ground floor, and a great chamber and two secondary bedchambers on the first floor. (Internally the stonework reflects this usage: it is functional in the basement and rises in decorative quality as you ascend.) The southern arm of the cross was meant to contain a staircase. Some of the internal woodwork may have been completed before building work stopped, but Cromwell's men filched the timber. Little has happened to the structure since. It is extraordinary to think of this superb building as a garden accessory, a luxury, an appendage. Its cubic capacity is that of a small modern mansion block. Its dimensions are not far off those

'Both house and water garden present themselves as an interrupted dream, an unfinished symphony, a grand plan suspended for ever by a change of fortune and the turn of personal and historical events.'

Mark Bradshaw

of the respectable villas designed by the fledgling architect John Nash around 1790 in the less wealthy world of the Tivyside community we'll encounter at Clynfyw (see page 145). Yet, as architectural historian Mark Girouard wrote in his guidebook to Lyveden, lodges like this were 'built in a holiday or fanciful spirit'. The Treshams and their friends would plan to decamp there for entertaining, or when the business of the main house got too much for them.

With Sir Thomas the spirit was more than just fanciful. He used the building as a declaration of his faith. This is evident in the cross-shape and the decorative metopes. But the symbolism goes far, far deeper than this, and yet can entirely escape our notice. The shape and dimensions of the whole building, the numbers of its sides, the facets of its window bays, are all calculated on the basis of religiously significant numbers. Its plan is the equilateral shape of a Greek cross, made up of five equal squares. Other measurements and multiples play on the figures of three for the Trinity (as in the Rushton lodge); five is the number of both Jesus and Mary, and represents the Wounds of Christ; seven, the number of the Godhead, symbolizes the Instruments of the Passion, the Stages of the Cross and so on. And who, without prompting, would think to measure the perimeter of each wing and discover that it measured 81 feet, which is three times three times three times three? Or know that this was significant?

And apart from all this, the Lodge is a superb piece of classical architecture. At his death Tresham's vast library was catalogued and shown to contain one of the finest collections of architectural works in England. Books by Alberti, de l'Orme, Palladio, Serlio, Vitruvius and de Vries, among others, demonstrate the pedigree of his ambitious building schemes.

An Elizabethan Garden Picture

Interest has always focused on the lodge. It is only comparatively recently that a parallel concern for garden history and archaeology has manifested itself. The remains of the Lyveden garden, with its parterre, terraces, pyramidal and spiral mounts, and an elaborate system of canals, are a rare survival of the great water gardens that were such an important, and delightful, feature of the most spectacular gardens of around 1600.

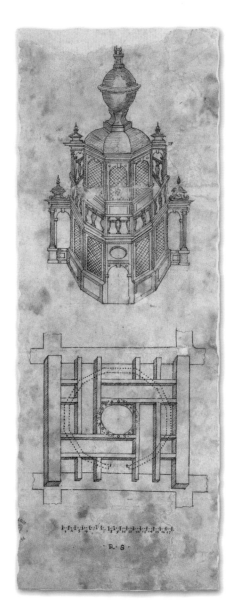

Robert Stickells's drawing for a central lantern or cupola was found among Tresham's papers. (Stickells was the surveyor who designed the classical entablature in which Tresham's men carved the metopes.) Set atop a galleried second floor, the cupola would have given the New Bield an extraordinarily ornate and grandiose roofline.

The eastern end of the terrace with its 'truncated' or pyramidal mount is remarkably well preserved. Until recently the clear outlines of these historic features were masked in vegetation. Elaborate water gardens with terraced walks were typical of late Elizabethan and Jacobean gardens made by wealthy landowners, but few have survived anywhere.

The complete extent of the terrace between the two pyramidal mounts fills the horizon above the newly planted orchard. Its outline draws the visitor to investigate, but gives no hint of the elaborate water gardens that lie beyond.

Sir Thomas was nothing if not a man of his age. The wealthy courtiers who were his contemporaries were studding the map of Britain with conspicuous constructions, invariably surrounded by elaborate garden settings, like the splendid collars and ruffs framing those enigmatic, worldly Tudor faces. Fine houses and fine gardens are created in ages that 'grow to civility and elegancy' as Francis Bacon wrote in 1597, the year Tresham was imprisoned at Ely. Tresham is a rare example of an ordinary landed gentleman – rather than a nobleman – who came to 'build stately' as well as to 'garden finely' (to borrow Bacon's words) in his combination of a striking building and an ambitious garden layout. Lyveden still exhibits the structures of many of the larger gardens of the time, including those at Hampton Court and Hatfield, at Theobalds and at the Northamptonshire palaces of Kirby and Holdenby. Bacon's own garden at Gorhambury in Hertfordshire had elaborate water features. Apart from remnants, such as those at Bindon Abbey in Dorset, little if any of these gardens survives in an original state, demonstrating the enormous significance of Lyveden in studying this evolutionary period of garden design. Both the sheer scale of the human engineering works and the state of preservation make the garden unique. It has no real parallels, and the twin 'truncated' pyramidal mounts at either end of the terrace between the water garden and the orchard are the only surviving examples of this form of garden design. They remain exceptionally well preserved.

'Preservation' and 'conservation' are words preferred by Custodian Mark Bradshaw, rather than the more interventionist terminology of 'restoration'. His own title, with its connotations of care and protection, seems perfectly in tune with the language of Sir Thomas and the site: 'property manager' sounds altogether too modern and active, and 'gardener' not quite right, although with further advances, active gardening may become a bigger part of the job.

Gardening at Lyveden tends to be of a woody nature. Nowadays it involves a lot of hedge-laying, with the orchard project promising further woody work. It started with clearing the overgrown trees and scrub, which had grown back since the initial inter- vention of the National Trust's Acorn Campers in the 1970s. At first you couldn't see the mounts for the trees, and the full extent of the water systems could only be guessed at by a casual onlooker, although the outlines of the features had been formally recorded by archaeology many years earlier. Progress in this part of

'Lodges were often built in a fanciful or holiday spirit.'

Mark Girouard

the garden has been deliberately slow and gradual, a process of discovery, uncovering the neglected earthworks from their mantle of trees and scrub and revealing the extent of the canals. A few years ago they appeared no more than a series of discrete pockets of water inter- spersed with marshy patches of willow scrub. The canals never were completed to form a square. The western side overlays another piece

In spring the mounts are studded with wild flowers that Tresham would have considered useful as well as ornamental, including primroses, violets and hellebores. The bulbs of the bluebell (which he might have known as 'English jacinth') were a source of glue used in making books and for fletching arrows.

of archaeology – part of a medieval moated site – and for some reason Tresham's men did not dig it out. (They can hardly have been delayed for purposes of archaeology, as is often the case nowadays.) The recent work has been done by hand (and the occasional chainsaw) by Mark Bradshaw and a hard-working volunteer, Bob Oakley, a retired landscape manager and horticulturalist for the Development Corporation. Scrub clearance can be very therapeutic. Modern earth-moving equipment was brought in only for the task of removing silt from the moats.

To work with old tools, such as axes and saws, on a site like this is to feel some communion with the bodies who laboured here in the past. The largest of the trees on the terraces and mounts must be descended by several generations from any Tresham planted, and others will be weeds, but there is continuity nonetheless. Old fruit trees within the moated garden are believed to be direct descendants. The wildflowers that stud the grass in spring may be derived from original plantings – as could the prickly butcher's broom (*Ruscus aculeatus*) with its bristly messages from the shambles of the past. The butchers who sold the mutton from Tresham's sheep would have used it to scrub their blocks and to protect the meat from mice.

The transition from the sublime to the mundane is one that gardeners constantly make. We find another parallel in Tresham as a man of his time. To the Elizabethan mind things spiritual and celestial were quite as concrete as stones and mortar. The cosmic world order, the four elements, the theological scheme of sin and salvation were as real as the weather and the seasons. We can imagine him sitting in prison picturing in his mind's eye exactly what he wanted built, elaborating his numerological games for the dimensions and decoration of his buildings, imbuing every inch with spiritual significance, adding his own complex layers of encrypted symbolism. And at the same time he was instructing the masons on what stone to use for different parts of the building and calculating the run-off of his drainage channels ('the great sink' was to fall '6 inches in every 10 yards'). We know all this because we have these detailed specifications in his own words.

Hidden Papers

It is every restorer's dream to have a horde of original documents to comb for clues. A gift from the spirits of the past. Some of Sir

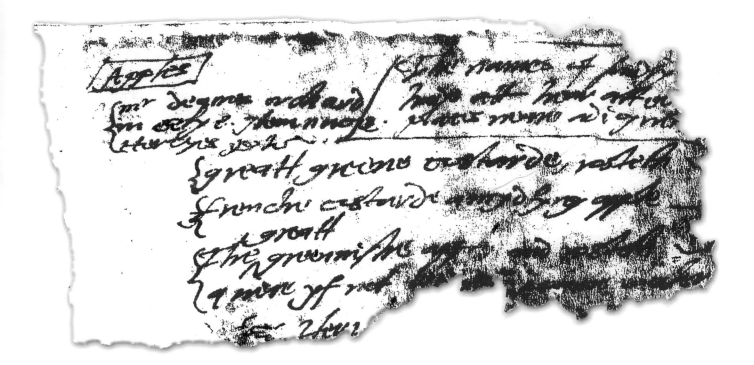

Thomas's came to light at Rushton Hall in 1832. Workmen making alterations removed a lintel from an ancient doorway and discovered a secret alcove – a kind of priest's hidey-hole – containing a bundle of old papers and books, several of which were Roman Catholic works. There were bills and letters, some of which related to those memorable events of 5 November 1605. A month after Sir Thomas Tresham died in September that year, his son Francis became embroiled in the Gunpowder Plot. He was arrested on 12 November, was attainted as a traitor and died in the Tower two days before Christmas. Francis had always been a hot-headed lad, often in debt and occasionally in serious trouble. His participation in Essex's rebellion in 1601 brought a fine of £2000, besides costing his father £1000 in a bribe to the powerful Lady Katherine (whose husband, Sir Thomas Howard, later became Earl of Suffolk) to use her influence to stop Francis being charged with treason.

Interesting as these matters are (and Lyveden would make a marvellous setting for commemorative *son et lumière* performances of watery masques and fireworks displays), we gardeners have more pertinent leads to follow.

The richest documentary clue to the Lyveden garden is the letter Sir Thomas wrote from Ely on 9 October 1597. It was written to John

The handwriting in Tresham's letter from Ely is tricky to decipher, even where the paper is undamaged. Here is the top part of the page listing the fruits he intends to plant in his orchard. Under the heading 'Apples' is a note mentioning his principal source – 'Mr deans orchard in Ely...' – and below that he specifies the names 'greatt greene custarde', 'french custarde' and 'the greatt greenish apple'.

Slynne and alludes frequently to George Levens. Both men worked for Tresham at his main seat of Rushton Hall and at the old Manor House at Lyveden. Between them they seem to have carried out the work on the New Bield. They organized the earth-moving, hired skilled staff and supervised transport of stone from appropriate quarries.

The letter runs to some 16 sides of densely written script. It contains detailed instructions for laying out the garden, as well as listing specific plants – mostly trees. Deciphering Tresham's writing presents a considerable challenge. He wrote in a barely intelligible hand in English, Latin and French, and had a habit of finishing one side of a sheet of paper, then turning it upside down and beginning on the other side. Clare Bense, the volunteer historian who has been going through his copious notes, reports that before you can even begin to guess at the subject of his letters, you have to figure out which way up the writing is, and what language it's in. Some of the words and phrases have been lost where the paper is damaged. However, what remains reveals Sir Thomas to have been endowed with a meticulously practical mind, as assiduous in his garden planning as he was in his farming and building plans. He was a down-to-earth landscape architect, as well as a knowledgeable plantsman.

Tresham specified the dimensions of the garden plot 'wherein my garden lodge now standeth'. It was to be staked out to 108 yards square (numbers enthusiasts might like to seek out some significance in this figure) and planted with twin rows of quickset hedging raised on banks to make 'a private walk' around the garden. Tresham sometimes specified the height and breadth of the hedges but left some measurements to his correspondent's 'discretions', as long as it was 'workmanly done'. He was keen for the hedging to be planted 'while the lodge is in building. Hereby the building will be well fenced in, and the hedges well grown up, before the lodge be finished, and the garden perfected.' We should consider what this implies. The lodge would be encountered not (as it is now) standing on a flat open platform, but rising beyond a framework of hedging.

Sir Thomas knew exactly what he wanted, and what he didn't want. He urged Slynne to shape the plants to ensure that his arbour hedges didn't 'grow thin at the bottom' or leggy. He projected eight large arbours for ornaments and for planting: 'Some of them may be converted to gardening as wherein to keep choicest flowers... But this

may hereafter [be] considered of.' How satisfying it would be to find out what he considered to be 'choicest flowers'! Elsewhere he mentions planting 'roses both damask and red', but this sounds less like ornamental than useful planting. Rose petals had many uses apart from scenting the air in a garden. Gerard's *Herbal* (1597) compares damask roses favourably with other types, being 'of a more pleasant smel, and fitter for meat and medicine'. Tresham adds that the 'dropping of roses will hinder nothing growing under them', specifying 'herbs, strawberries or the like', further suggesting a practical attitude.

Gardeners must appreciate Tresham's down-to-earth practicality: gardening is not only about choosing pleasing plants and laying out an attractive design, but making the garden work as a place to be in. 'The

Garden sites may contain layer upon layer of history. Tresham's 400-year-old unfinished garden was not built on virgin land, but near the remains of a medieval moated settlement lying to the northwest. Some of the medieval ditches are now being cleared of weed trees.

From the terrace the replanted orchard falls away downhill towards the Old Bield, now a private house.

answer lies in the soil,' as they used to say. At Lyveden it is water-retentive chalky clay. Tresham paid a good deal of attention to the unglamorous subjects of water supply, drainage and maintenance. Planning that most fashionable item, a bowling green, to the north of the lodge, he was anxious that the grass on the green be 'kept very short with oft mowing'. He had no intention of allowing visitors in his open or 'close' walks to get their feet wet. Paths were to be either of grass, or of gravel with sound stone foundations a foot thick. His specifications for his walks and alleys could be followed by quantity surveyors today.

Tresham's Trees

Tresham planned a great deal of tree planting, as the Ely letter shows. Birch arbours, groves of oak and ash, elms, sycamores, walnut tree walks – both ornamental trees and fruit were to be staked to keep them upright and to prevent root-rock. He was even particular about 'husbandry in stakes'. Baking them in the fire would straighten them and make them last longer, 'and as they decay in length by reason of too much rotting as doth stand in the ground, so will they notwithstanding serve smaller trees, from one to another until they be not a foot long'. How many of us look after our bamboo canes that carefully?

Fruit grown from seed included pears, cider and crab apples, cherries – and walnuts, which deserved special attention. Tresham believed a walnut tree fruited better when grafted, 'though it be but grafted with itself'. Some of his black cherries were also grafted. We gardeners can imagine the frustrated prisoner fretting about the welfare of the plants in his absence. He pictured the cherries sown in his nursery suffering a check in growth through becoming overcrowded – 'they should be thinned by choice drawing away the slenderest of them…have the fairest and greatest stand unremoved that hereafter they may be removed into my moated orchard'. The thinnings were to be planted on, to catch up in due course.

It is in the orchard at Lyveden New Bield that 'restoration' in its most active sense can be found.

During his detention at Ely, Sir Thomas became well acquainted with the varieties of fruit grown in the dean's orchard, opposite his prison in the bishop's palace. The page on which he wrote his list is

Trees for Sir Thomas's Orchard

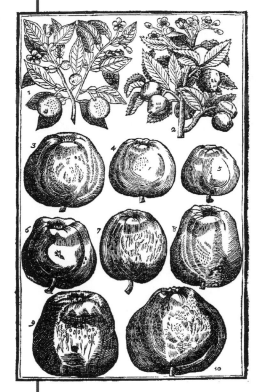

APPLES

Catshead – box-shaped. Cooks to a sharp, firm purée, or is made into dumplings and taken into the fields.

Doctor Harvey's – cooks to a purée; slow-baked, makes a highly flavoured sweetmeat dessert that will keep for a week or more.

French Crab (also called Ironsides) – cooks to a sharp purée; loses its acidity around New Year and becomes rather bland. Renowned for keeping.

Golden Harvey (sometimes called the Brandy Apple) – small, golden russeted; intensely flavoured sweet/sharp, aromatic. The high specific gravity of the juice makes strong cider. Tresham noted that 'Harvey's apple' kept till Candlemas (2 February).

Green Custard – costard type, having ribbed shape, similar to 'Catshead', but maturing earlier. Sharp, plain-tasting dessert fruit. Tresham also noted this as the 'Greatt Greene Custarde'.

Old Pearmain – a pear-shaped apple, richly flavoured.

Winter Queening – early English. Bright yellow, sweet/sharp flavour. Sweetness increases with keeping; suitable for desserts. Cooked slices retain their shape. Tresham described it as 'a middling apple, somewhat large' and noted that it would keep until Lent.

PEARS

Black Worcester – the pear on the Worcester coat of arms, found in the county during Tudor times. Perhaps the original Warden Pear from Warden Abbey, Bedfordshire. Keeps until February.

Windsor – early variety. May have been the pear growing on Windsor Hill, planted by the royals

PLUM FAMILY

Cherry Plum
Common Damson
Orleans
Shepherd's Bullace

Shropshire Damson
  (or Prune Damson)
Transparent Gage

rather more badly damaged than the rest of the Ely letter (see page 27). Not only is the paper more fragmented, but unfamiliar names tend to be even harder to decipher than straightforward prose. The note 'Mr dean' punctuates the list with extraordinary frequency, suggesting perhaps that the dean's orchard might have been seen as the source of supply for grafting material.

Armed with some of the names specified by Sir Thomas, Mark Bradshaw approached the Brogdale Horticultural Trust at Faversham in Kent, whose 60 acres of orchards are home to the National Fruit Collections. They specialize in conserving old varieties of fruit, and were able to provide several of the original varieties – enough to mean that the orchard would be planted in the spirit Sir Thomas intended.

Wardens and Walnuts, Crabs and Costards

Few of the fruit names are familiar. Warden pears were larger and harder than other types and regarded almost as a different fruit. Costards were correspondingly large, ribbed apple varieties, sold by barrow boys who later became known as costermongers. In the plum family were gages, damsons and bullaces. Morello cherries and walnuts (*Juglans regia*) are also on the Lyveden planting list.

Once again, it's worth stepping back in time to the world in which Sir Thomas lived. Having a good range of fruit was partly a matter of status, partly one of necessity. Walnuts, for example, were valued not only for their nutritious nut, but also for the medicinal uses of their leaves, which were supposed to cure chilblains, acne and swollen glands, among other complaints. Pears symbolized good health, fortune and hope, and had a binding quality supposed to stem bleeding and diarrhoea. Cherries were fruits of Paradise, with many soothing and rejuvenating properties. Plums, ruled by Venus, were, according to the herbalist Thomas Culpeper, 'like women – some better, some worse', whereas when dried as prunes they might 'loosen the belly, procure appetite and cool the stomach'.

The virtues and value of apples are less fanciful to us today. Apple orchards played a vital part in gardens, and their orderly productiveness was a source of pleasure. You needed not just fresh fruit for the table but for drying, for wines and juices, for cooking in numerous ways plain and fancy, for the sustenance of the workforce as well as the family. It

Herb-rich grassland studded with flowers, such as campion and plantain, is more in keeping with Sir Thomas's time than the monocultures sown by modern farmers. The National Trust has also established a wildflower meadow to the west of the New Bield.

is only in the last couple of generations that we have become used to buying fruit in the supermarket all year round. Self-sufficient gardeners who grow food to eat still know their apples, and tread in the footsteps of Sir Thomas. They know exactly what varieties to plant together for cross-pollination at the right time, and when each will be ready to harvest and to eat – not the same thing. They store them carefully and use them according to their keeping qualities. They tend not to reckon these in the same terms as Sir Thomas – Michaelmas, Candlemas, Lent and so on – but no doubt look after them in the same cool, airy lofts and wage the same war on mice and mould.

Custodian Mark Bradshaw uses an enlarged plan to explain developments on the site to a party of visitors.

The experts at Brogdale helped build a picture of how Tresham's apples might have been served. Apples were an important feature of desserts. French dessert apples and wet and dry apple desserts were accorded the same importance as the more exotic fruits. The 19th-century pomologist Robert Hogg said that transparent green sweetmeats could be made from small, immature codlins with a delicious flavour, similar to a green apricot. (Codlin or codling is a name now applied to a variety of apple elongated towards the eye; then it was any hard apple inedible unless cooked, or, indeed, any immature apple.) Displays of apples were important on the tables of the wealthy, as well as in special recipes, such as butters, creams, fools and possets. Pippin creams, for example, were made by cooking the fruit with orange flower water and sugar, then mixing them with eggs and cream. Syllabubs made with cider or apple pulp were thickened with egg yolks, flavoured with rosewater and sprinkled with ginger and cinnamon. Served in small glasses, these exotic creations were devised to impress guests.

While on this mouthwatering subject, perhaps we should also remember what a comparative luxury sugar was. By Sir Thomas's day most came from North Africa, imported by the Barbary Company or, more often, as prize cargoes captured by English privateers. It cost a shilling a pound – the equivalent of the day's wage of a craftsman.

Restoration is not all serious archaeology and grind. You can have fun, and you can come across strange juxtapositions. If the ghost of Sir Thomas had deigned to revisit his orchard one morning in late January 2002 he might have found himself in some familiar company.

The venue was the rectangle of ground just downhill from the terrace and its framing pyramidal mounts. Planting began here around 1600 – as aerial photographs and soil samples have proved. After Sir Thomas's death in 1605 his estate was faced with considerable debts, and the orchard was called on to pay some of them. In 1609 Lady Tresham offered Robert Cecil 50 fruit trees from Lyveden for the gardens at Hatfield, in a letter that casts a touching sidelight on the scene: 'Because I think no one can furnish you with more and better trees and of a fitter growth than this ground, for my late husband, as he did take great delight, so did he come to great experience and judgement therein.'

A boating party is organized to reach the middle of the moat. Here core samples of silt will be taken. Pollen grains should be well preserved in the organic mud. Troops from 39 Engineer Regiment are called in to lend a hand.

In an attempt to rewind the spools of time, members of the Tudor Group (specialists in period re-enactment from Gloucestershire) came along in authentic period costume to help plant the new fruit trees. (There were anachronisms: they arrived thanks to the internal combustion engine and were recorded by photography.) There is something timeless about the human figure poised with one foot lifted ready to drive a spade into the ground. Illustrations in various editions of books such as Thomas Hill's *Gardener's Labyrinth* and other woodcuts of the 16th and 17th centuries showing everyday gardening jobs have the same familiarity. The Tudor Group used wooden spades tipped with iron. It was a good publicity stunt, raising public awareness of the site, but also fulfilled another remit – giving the public a little educational nudge about our forgotten past when tasks were measured by horse-power and manpower.

(Mark Bradshaw had earlier made use of a giant petrol-driven mechanical auger to prepare the 306 tree-planting holes in the 5-acre site, and also carted manure using a tractor and trailer. You can take authenticity too far.)

Then there was the boating party, another anachronism. The mission was to get into mid-moat to take a series of core samples of the sediment for pollen analysis. Serious stuff, not intrinsically photogenic. The BBC wanted to make a splash, so they called in the army. These were none of your pensive Elizabethan swains, though they'd no doubt have shown many a finely turned calf if they'd been allowed to dress in doublet and hose, and might have been persuaded to adopt the appropriate melancholy demeanour of the chaps portrayed in miniatures by Nicholas Hilliard or Isaac Oliver. Personnel from 39 Engineer Regiment, based at Waterbeach Barracks, Cambridge, came along with their boat and their lifejackets and ferried our scientist to selected spots where probe and corer were plunged into the watery depths.

Specialists at the department of Geological Sciences at the University of Huddersfield analysed one of the samples in detail. By identifying the sequence of pollen grains, algae and other organic particles, such as microscopic fragments of charcoal (perhaps from stubble burning), experts can build up a picture of fluxes in agriculture and land use. Occasionally the samples also give a hint of actual gardening activity.

The deepest sediment showed evidence of grassland with herbs such as sheep's sorrel and bird's-foot trefoil – a confirmation of Sir Thomas Tresham's sheep walks surrounding the site. A picture emerges of the new garden around the moat as an area of bare soil planted with trees, including willows and plums, and colonized by opportunist weeds. Deposits of pollen from herbaceous plants are non-specific, and could be from garden plants or from native wildflowers.

Subsequent layers of sediment reflect changes in the wider landscape: 'gardening' is less evident than the rise and fall of woodland

A sausage of sediment from the moat is disgorged from the piston corer to be sent for analysis. Its profile will tell the story of the surrounding landscape since the digging of the moat.

and hedges, phases when marsh plants indicate poor drainage (perhaps parts of the moat had silted up); and changes in agriculture, from the early 19th-century boom to the 'Dig for Victory' campaign of World War II.

This is not ground-breaking stuff, but it is a satisfying confirmation of what we know of the site from other sources. In recording changes in farming practices, it also sounds a warning note. The last traces of lost gardens and their vital landscape settings can all too easily be ploughed up, and inconvenient (but irreplaceable) earthworks ripped out with unwanted hedgerows. There was a mount at Rushton, originally topped by a statue of Hercules. The statue disappeared long ago, but the mount was bulldozed away only in the 1940s.

'…in gloom monastic, buried deep/'Midst shadowy trees, and lone sequester'd fields/ Thy ruins, Liveden, still majestic stand.'

Thomas Bell, *Rural Album* (1847)

As a garden in the landscape, Lyveden New Bield has been overlooked and passed by, but it has never been forgotten. And in 'modern' gardening history, as long ago as 1979, Lyveden was given three-quarter-page coverage in the monumental *Gardens of the National Trust* by Graham Stuart Thomas, then Gardens Consultant to the Trust. He wrote that the remains represented the oldest garden layout owned by the Trust, and one of the oldest in the country anywhere. Then he warned: 'But do not go there thinking to see an old garden; there is little but mounts, earthen banks, canals and the shell of the unfinished New Bield in the midst of quiet, open fields.' Today's visitors will see a little more identifiable gardening activity and find a more active appreciation of Lyveden's presence as a garden.

Graham Thomas also alluded to the unfathomable nature of Sir Thomas's intentions, to which he found no answer: 'The only sounds are the soughing of the wind in the trees and the croaking of the moorhens.'

Lyveden New Bield is stark in silhouette and in moat-reflection. Had Sir Thomas Tresham built his projected cupola, his successors would have seen an altogether more wonderful reflection.

Bleak solitude or romantic melancholy? Do not be discouraged from finding out. To stand beneath the wide sky beside the New Bield is to feel the presence of the past and of something else. Whether it is some inkling of Sir Thomas's Christian message or some other mystery, it is up to you to decide.

ABERGLASNEY
The Case of the Cloister Conundrum

'The report of my death was an exaggeration,' Mark Twain announced on hearing that his obituary had been published. Aberglasney might claim similar fame. Its demise was prematurely foretold in *Lost Houses of Wales* (1986) by Thomas Lloyd, which described some 400-odd properties that had disappeared through accident or design, or were currently crumbling through neglect. Among that number was many a monstrosity, but also some rare and handsome examples of period style or vernacular building, whose loss was greatly to be mourned. Aberglasney belongs to neither of these extremes. Architecture has never been Aberglasney's strong point, as it has Lyveden's, yet an astonishing effort has been made to save it. It has been rescued and restored for the sake not of its house but for part of its garden.

Ideally a restoration project is achieved by means of triangulating a number of datum points. Evidence on the ground is corroborated by documentary sources, and the garden you find corresponds in style to what you might expect to have been created at that place and time. That's in a perfect world. Aberglasney is far from that, and the Cloister Garden that prompted its rescue and made it famous presents some of its trickiest puzzles.

Aberglasney and Lyveden New Bield were both in the making at about the same time. Having been forgotten or overlooked or 'lost', both are now acclaimed as rare survivals. But the contrast between the two places could not be more striking. Lyveden's story, like its lodge, is sharp in its detail and clearly outlined. The garden-maker Sir Thomas Tresham and his family hold a well-documented place in history, and a fair degree of consensus attends decisions about how to conserve and maintain Lyveden. Aberglasney, on the other hand, presents anything but a clear-cut case history. Its original makers are shadowy figures, and as successive generations rebuilt and altered both house and garden, they blurred traces of evidence. Fact is overlaid by myth and rumour. Documentation about the property is at best sketchy and has had a tendency to disappear.

An Outline of the Plot...

Aberglasney is the hub of a major garden history revolution that began in the mid-1980s when William Wilkins, architect-turned-painter, rallied interest in historic gardens of the picturesque Towy valley in particular. Among the results, apart from the rescue from oblivion of scores of old gardens, was the founding of the Welsh Historic Gardens Trust and the creation of the National Botanic Garden of Wales.

In 1995, for a nominal sum, the recently formed Aberglasney Restoration Trust purchased the Grade II* listed house and surrounding gardens – the derelict core of a modest gentry estate twice fragmented by sales since World War II. The property was little altered since its Victorian heyday, although vandalism and neglect had escalated decay in recent decades. Within the Victorian aggrandizement, two major building phases lay concealed: the house built by Bishop Rudd and his son in the early 1600s (of which only the cellar range remains intact), and the stylish Queen Anne 'improvements' set in hand by Robert Dyer in the early 1700s.

Since 1997, a high-profile programme of restoration and renovation has made Aberglasney one of the best known gardens in Wales. The Restoration Trust's approach is multi-faceted. The garden structures and walls have been faithfully restored and rebuilt. The north and west façades of the house have been renovated as a back-drop to the gardens. However, the planting around the pool, in the former kitchen gardens and the woodlands is a creative re-interpretation. Only in the Cloister Garden is there an attempt to return to the Jacobean status quo.

Aberglasney is all about water, and some of the rills that splash in the Pool Garden have travelled through the cellars of the house.

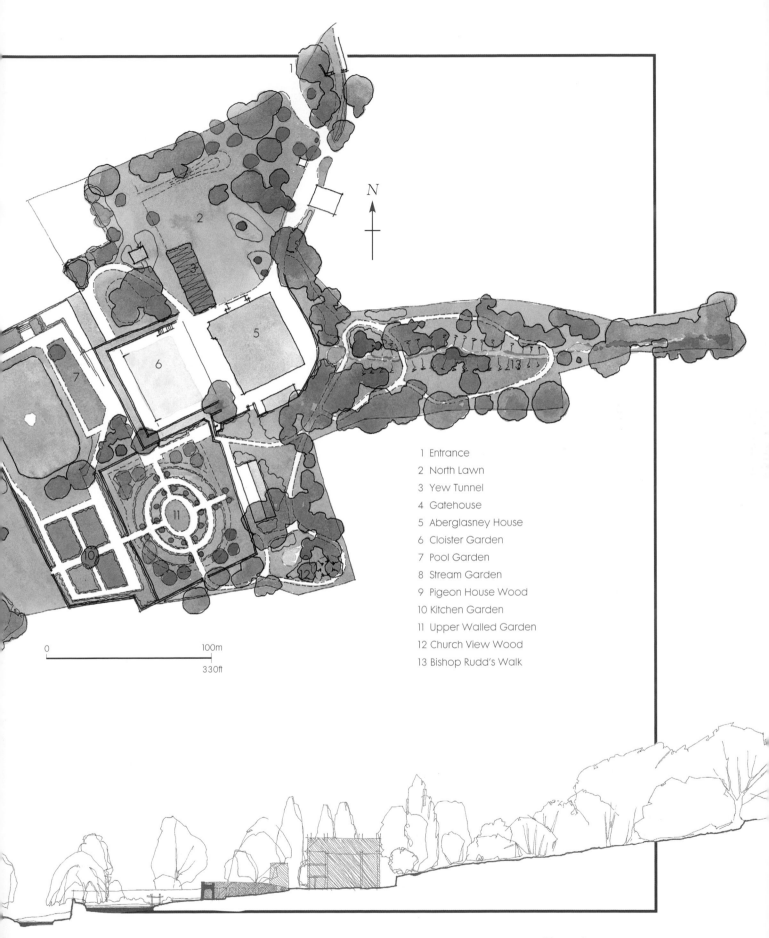

1 Entrance
2 North Lawn
3 Yew Tunnel
4 Gatehouse
5 Aberglasney House
6 Cloister Garden
7 Pool Garden
8 Stream Garden
9 Pigeon House Wood
10 Kitchen Garden
11 Upper Walled Garden
12 Church View Wood
13 Bishop Rudd's Walk

0   100m

330ft

We depend on archaeology to give us the dates of the Cloister Garden structures because they are not recorded in any contemporary documents that we know about. We depend on speculation to deduce what the garden-makers might have had in mind. It has taken dedicated archaeologists to pinpoint the date of its making to a span of three decades or so at the beginning of the 17th century. Since we know the identity of the two generations who owned Aberglasney at the time, the obvious course of action is to try to find out what kind of gardening ambitions these people might entertain. The two presumed garden-makers are Bishop Anthony Rudd (about whom the only thing everybody remembers is that he fell foul of Elizabeth I) and his younger son and heir Sir Rice Rudd. It is possible to sketch an outline of their lives and activities, but their ideas and motives are singularly hard to pin down. The more so since they lived in a period of unprecedented experimentation in garden-making. When kings and courtiers all over the land were constructing grandiose garden schemes influenced by a flurry of new ideas from the Continent, who can say how an ambitious gentleman might decide to flaunt his new wealth and taste?

All this makes the challenge of restoration a considerable one. There are as many contrasting ideas about what should be done as there are conflicting theories of interpretation.

A Speculative Scenario

In 1594 Anthony Rudd DD, Dean of Gloucester, is elevated to the bishopric of St David's on the westernmost tip of the most westerly part of Wales. When he travels between London, Gloucester and his new diocese, whether he follows the route that is now the A40, via Raglan (with its fashionable castle gardens) and Brecon (with its bishop), or whether he chooses the more southerly A48 and M4 via potentially visitable places such as Chepstow, Llandaff and Margam, he finds himself passing through the ancient town of Carmarthen, which, incidentally, has a bishop's palace. He starts buying up land hereabouts and reaping the tithes. He's a good bishop but makes a bad impression on Elizabeth I, so his expected career success is checked. He petitions Sir Robert Cecil in vain for the sees of Hereford and Norwich when they fall vacant between 1601 and 1603. Then a new king, James I, comes to the throne and the Bishop is back in royal favour.

Aberglasney holds no brief for period authenticity in planting most of the grounds, just excellence. Aberglasney director Graham Rankin is an expert on magnolias, and *M. loebneri* 'Merrill' is a beautiful recent cultivar.

But something has changed. For reasons unknown, some of the land he has acquired in Llangathen parish takes his fancy. It belonged to Sir William Thomas, who sold up when he married an heiress and moved to North Wales. (The documents are missing, but Sir William was in his new home by 1605.) On or near the site of the old 'place' of the Thomas family, Plas Llangathen, Bishop Rudd begins to build, and constructs a house containing a chapel with an ornate pulpit. (This is still on record as being there in the 1780s.) He extends the parish church to accommodate the elaborate tomb that his wife erects to him after his death in 1614. He makes charitable provision in perpetuity for almshouses for four local men 'so poor, aged or decrepit' as to have no other means of support.

Usually a garden provides a setting for a house. At Aberglasney the situation is reversed, and the architecturally unremarkable building has been restored as a backdrop to the historically important garden. The north façade is Queen Anne, updated with a portico early in Queen Victoria's reign.

We can only speculate about why Anthony Rudd decided to put down roots here. It's a pleasant spot. Perhaps Plas Llangathen suits his elevated station, and its views over the lazy, generous Towy valley and of more distant barren upland remind him of Yorkshire. He has a triangulation of distinguished neighbours in Dynevor to the east and Golden Grove to the south. His wife and younger son, Rice, seem at home here. This son marries first a Pembrokeshire lady (and three of their six children marry into Welsh families). Rice, apparently, continues his father's building spree.

By Faith Divided

Bishop Rudd was an almost exact contemporary of Sir Thomas Tresham, and the two had much in common. Rudd went to Cambridge, Tresham to Oxford. Both were religious men, for whom the arcane symbolism of numerology was a matter of practical faith. Both came from relatively modest backgrounds (though the Rudds, minor gentry from Easby in North Yorkshire, were fast outstripped by the Treshams in upward mobility) and made a name for themselves in the highest circles. Each enjoyed the favour of Queen Elizabeth and then lost it in expressing his faith. Each found a kind of reprieve when James I succeeded her in 1603.

'... the word "Glasne", a noun made by adding -ne to glas, *is the name of a river. In the language of Welsh landscape,* glas *means both 'blue' and 'green', like the colour of hills and waters. The estate lies close to the confluence,* aber, *of blue-greenness,* glasne, *of several streams:* Aber-glasne.'

Gillian Clarke,
Nine Green Gardens

Of course, as an eminent Anglican clergyman, Rudd was on the opposite side to Tresham on the question of recusants, who continued to trouble the bishopric of St David's well into the 1600s. When Anthony Rudd was Dean of Gloucester he was directed to receive into his house 'a verie obstinate Recusant, Margrett Throckmorton', daughter of Sir Thos. Throckmorton, Knt, 'for a tyme to comitt her to your charge to be conferred withall for her conformitie'. No suspected Papist was to be allowed to converse with her, and she was particularly to be kept apart from her mother, who was detained elsewhere. Was this Margaret any relation to Meriel Throckmorton, who married Sir Thomas in about 1566? It would be interesting to find out whether the

Rudds and the Treshams had any other less contentious mutual acquaintances. The Rudds had relatives in Northamptonshire. The Bishop's grandson, also named Anthony, married his distant cousin Judith, daughter of Thomas Rudd of Higham Ferrers, in that county.

We have the dashing portrait of Tresham in his armour (see page 16), but we know of no picture of the Bishop. There were once family portraits, but – if they have not been destroyed, or become impossible to recognize – it is unlikely that their present owners know the identity of the sitters. The nearest we can get is the defaced image of Bishop Rudd on its bedstead tomb in Llangathen parish church, its nose knocked off by Cromwell's men along with his ring-finger. It was erected to his memory by his widow in 1616. The drapery of the effigies is beautifully moulded and it would make sense for the physical likeness to be equally realistic. Rudd's face looks thin and sunken beneath prominent cheekbones, as if it were taken from a death mask.

The Gatehouse is thought to date from the time of the Rudds and was once flanked by buildings that formed part of a courtyard range. Later owners retained the tower as a folly that hinted at antiquity, and someone embellished its north-facing archway with a piece of recycled ecclesiastical moulding from similar motives.

Like Tresham, Rudd had a library of books, but his was not catalogued. He had pictures and maps, but we don't know what became of them. Sir Rice's youngest daughter, Constance, mentioned portraits in her will of 1672: one of her grandmother, the Bishop's wife, born Anne Dalton; one of Sir Rice, and one of Mary Magdalene. What became of them? The excerpt from Constance Rudd's will goes like this: 'Item I doe give and bequeath unto my nephew Sir Rice Rudd of Aberglasney Knight and Baronett son and heir of my brother Anthony Rudd deceased two hundred pounds of lawfull English money… I doe give and bequeath unto the said Sir Rice Rudd my grandmother's picture, my father's picture and Mary Magdalene's picture but in case Sir Rice Rudd should leave no heir male behind him lawfully begotten of his owne body Then I doe bequeath these three pictures to my nephew Anthony Rudd the son of my brother Thomas Rudd deceased.'

Was Mary Magdalene, patron saint of penitents, some kind of talisman? A picture of her owned by the Rudds was mentioned in Constance Rudd's will, and hers is the image carved in the central leg of the communion table in Llangathen parish church – a table that is supposed to have come from Bishop Rudd's long-lost chapel at Aberglasney. It is a strangely robust, primitive, almost pagan figure in the dark oak, clutching the jar of ointment that is her signature. Another characteristic is the long hair with which Mary wiped Christ's feet. The 17th-century ringleted ladies who were Rice Rudd's contemporaries wore their hair in 'repenter curls'.

Disappearing Documents

Aberglasney still makes fleeting appearances in popular books published today reiterating tales of ghosts and ghostly portents, such as corpse candles (disembodied lights that, according to local superstition, foretell deaths). It was first written about long ago. The 'nine green gardens' of an early owner were celebrated by the 15th-century poet Lewis Glyn Cothi in a horticultural reference rare in a Welsh praise-poem. The description predates the current layout, and the number (three times three) is probably a poetic conceit; but that does not stop people trying to count Aberglasney's various garden spaces. Still, it's a nice touch of gardening pedigree from the mists of time. For the past two and a half centuries Aberglasney has been famous for being the home of John Dyer, the poet and not-very-good painter whose resonant word-pictures describing his response to nature foreshadowed the Picturesque appreciation of landscape. 'Grongar Hill', his best-known poem, depicts the view to the west of Aberglasney; his poem 'The Country Walk' alludes to Aberglasney's 'gardens trim and terrace walks'. Both were published in 1726.

'Garden history is about people; it is indeed a branch of anthropology.'

Caroline Palmer

Two good accounts of the Rudds were published in the 20th century, but both are flawed. The first is an excellent article on 'Aberglasney and Its Families' by Francis Jones who, as County Archivist, wrote amusingly and informatively about Carmarthenshire. However, he often omitted to cite his sources and made a number of tantalizing statements whose origins are impossible to follow up. Where are the documents he used?

The second is the chapter about our Carmarthenshire Rudds in a book tracing the family all over Britain. Like Francis Jones, its author,

M.A. Rudd, occasionally muddled the names and numbers of off-spring. She was also confused about the origins of the structures she found at Aberglasney. She dated the 'ancient entrance gateway' to some 300 years before Bishop Rudd's rebuilding (it is now thought to be contemporary), and wrote that 'the lines of the present raised terrace walk certainly appear to be those of an ancient fortress wall'.

She also had terrible trouble with Welsh names. This is entirely understandable, as anyone who navigates through Wales reading road signs knows all too well – even today, when place names have been 'standardized'. Interpreting 17th-century phonetic transcriptions written in archaic script in imperfectly preserved documents is a challenge to the best scholars. All those places beginning with 'Llan–', for example, are almost always followed by the name of the saint to which the local church is dedicated. So Llangathen is named after one St Cathen – with a little initial mutation to further confuse the issue – and the nearby town of Llandeilo after St Teilo. Welsh saints are numerous and obscure. (It is almost as if they multiplied through gavelkind, that alternative to primogeniture by which property was divided between the children rather than left to the first-born, and is one reason why estates – and hidden gardens – in Wales have tended to be smaller and thicker on the ground than in England.)

Perhaps Mary Amelia Rudd's most unfortunate lapse is her mis-reading the name 'Assbody of Llanhithdd' for Aubrey, or Awbrey, of Llantrithyd. This is sad because she relished the element of serendipity in research and would have been delighted to trace a tenuous family link between the Rudds and the antiquarian John Aubrey, the author of *Brief Lives* and *Miscellanies* (1691) in which, incidentally, he relates Aberglasney's story of the five premonitory lights – five corpse candles – seen in the household of Sir Rice Rudd before five maids were found to have died in their beds overnight (see page 58). Aubrey seems unaware of any family connections.

More seriously, some documents dating from the Rudds' era disappeared relatively recently. They were in the possession of the Evans family, the last inheritors of the property before its sale in the 1950s. A visitor who claimed to be the royal calligrapher was shown them, and after he had departed the family realized the papers had disappeared too. Their trail was eventually traced across two continents but then went dead.

Aberglasney sits on the shoulder of the hill below Llangathen village and its 12th-century church dedicated to St Cathen. The footpath from the house to the church has always been known as Bishop Rudd's Walk.

Looking uphill from the Pool Garden, the tall outer wall of the Cloister Garden appears particularly impressive. The crenellations that decorate the top of the wall are suggestive of fortifications.

The documents must still exist somewhere. We should all keep our eyes peeled: perhaps an amnesty could be offered. The Aberglasney Restoration Trust and independent historians really do need to examine and transcribe them to find out if they contain any clues about the building of the house and the garden structures.

Numbers and the Bishop

Folk wisdom has it that Bishop Rudd disgraced himself. There's a cruelty in folk wisdom that likes to witness the high and mighty getting a comeuppance, a high churchman proving himself no holier than thou or I. Sex scandals and financial misdealing are particularly relished. But Bishop Rudd's misdemeanour was one of excessive ardour for the Queen's soul. It was perhaps tactless of him in his sermon preached at

Richmond in 1596 to formulate some of the phraseology that he advised Queen Elizabeth to use in her private meditations. To put into her mouth the words 'Behold I was borne in iniquitie, and in sinne hath my mother conceived me…' could be taken as a blanket allusion to original sin, or rather more personally by the daughter of Anne Boleyn. But it was Elizabeth's vanity that was most offended by the suggestion that she might confess: 'Lord, I have now put my foot within the doores of that age in which the Almond tree flourisheth; wherein men begin to car[r]y a Calendar in their bones, the senses begin to faile, the strength to diminish, yea all the powers of the body daily to decay.' The Queen was not amused. Three days after hearing Rudd's sermon Elizabeth proceeded to 'make herself merry with the standers-by' to emphasize just how keen her faculties were: 'Only to show how the good Bishop was deceived in supposing she was so decayed in her limbs and senses as he perhaps and others of that age were wont to be' – Bishop Rudd was 48 – 'she said she thanked God that neither her stomach or strength nor her voice for singing nor fingering instruments, nor, lastly her sight, was any whit decayed.'

Bishop Rudd himself used the word 'disgrace' in the sense of being 'out of favour' rather than being dishonoured: his hope was 'to encourage her in well doing, even by those speeches which proved so offensive'. He stayed out of the Queen's way and published the text of his sermon only in 1603.

The nub of the sermon, however, was its number-play. Three for the Trinity and the Heavenly Hierarchy; seven for the Sabbath, and seven times seven for a Jubilee; seven times nine for the climacterical year. Few people were expected to live beyond the age of 63, the Grand Climacteric. (According to Bishop Rudd, Elizabeth, born in September 1533, was supposed to pray, 'O Lord I am now entered a

Craig Hamilton is the architect who has designed the Cloister Garden restoration. Here is his elevation drawing for the final phase of the north range and its projected 'summer house', shown overgrown with ivy. For all Bishop Rudd's predilection for number-play, no rhyme or rhythm has been detected in the proportions of the Cloister Garden.

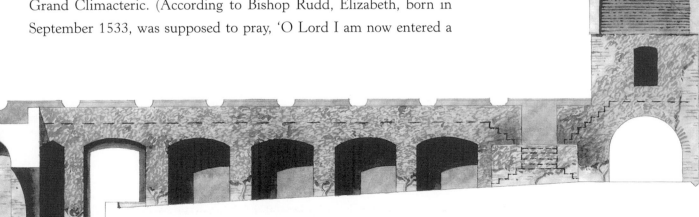

good way into the climacterical year of mine age which mine enemies wish and hope to be fateful unto me.') The number 88 was also rather threatening, but the Queen had ridden that one and emerged victorious over the Spanish Armada in 1588. With the cabbalistic 666 or Number of the Beast, Rudd said he could prove the Pope to be the Antichrist, but the Queen had heard enough.

Just as the biblical figures quoted were a matter of belief, so the numinous numbers themselves were as real as the things they represented. Who does this call to mind but Sir Thomas Tresham? But whereas Sir Thomas permeated the New Bield with his numerical symbolism, we can find no sign that the Reverend Father in God,

In the arches and alcoves of the Cloister Garden time slowly moulds the mortar into stalactites, drip by drip.

Anthony Rudd, Doctor of Divinity and Lord Bishop of St David's, followed suit when he laid out his plans for Aberglasney.

From someone as obsessed with numbers as Bishop Rudd, you'd expect some kind of numerical pattern.

John Phibbs is a garden historian who specializes in the Tudor period, and recently has acted as the Monitor who officially supervises work done for Heritage Lottery Fund grant aid at Aberglasney. Before he ever saw Aberglasney he had studied contemporary garden architecture and found it full of hidden logic and patterns, as Lyveden is. He'd explain how the mind-set of the period conceived structures in terms of a key measurement or matrix that you might find permeating the design and endowing it with significance for the maker. In theory, you'd seek this in the dimensions of Aberglasney's parapet walk – its height, breadth, the sizes of the archways, and in the multiples of this unit. No such thing. All the arches are different sizes and shapes. There is no symmetry. The cloister range corresponds to no mathematical pattern anyone can determine.

Mind you, Sir Rice has had a hand in what we find. Building went on beyond the Bishop's lifetime. Perhaps the initial intention was altered or blurred, or the early plans misplaced? Such a theory is unsatisfactory. As the 1600s progressed and Italian influence became stronger, you might expect more rather than less symmetry and order in garden architecture.

Enter Sir Rice

An impression that Rice Rudd, a younger son, was a mummy's boy is probably misplaced. It's just that his name invariably comes up linked with that of his mother as they administer the Bishop's estate after his death. The first-born, Anthony Rudd junior, was out of the picture in Gloucestershire, married to a wealthy bride no doubt lined up during Bishop Rudd's time as Dean of Gloucester. And then suddenly the elder son was dead, and Rice was heir to the fortune their father had accumulated. The untimely death of the first-born in his prime must have drawn comparisons with Henry, Prince of Wales, James I's son, who had died of typhoid fever in 1612 aged 18, and who would have reigned instead of Charles I had he lived. Both Bishop Rudd and Rice Rudd might have encountered Prince Henry at court, or known of his ambitious garden plans at Richmond Palace.

Along with his father, Sir Rice moved in circles where he might have encountered the Tresham family. Both frequented the court of James I. Lewis Tresham, Sir Thomas's second son, who inherited his

Archaeologist Kevin Blockley briefs Chris Beardshaw on the many puzzles and problems the Cloister Garden has posed. The sandstone loggia on the west façade behind them is one of the 19th-century embellishments to the house.

depleted estates, accompanied a royal party to Madrid when Prince Charles went a-wooing of a Spanish princess in 1623. Also of the party were Sir John Vaughan, Sir Rice's next-door neighbour at Golden Grove and Comptroller of the Household of the Prince of Wales, and his son Richard Vaughan.

Sir Rice's only definite garden contact we know about is Llantrithyd in the Vale of Glamorgan, a well-documented but now ruinous garden of the late 16th century, with strong similarities to Aberglasney. The raised terrace walks that Sir Rice must have paced as he made arrangements for the marriage of his daughter and courted his own second wife are still standing, although a thicket of weed-trees now makes them impossible to pace. Llantrithyd was owned by Sir Thomas Aubrey, father of Sir Rice's second wife, Elizabeth. He married her at the same time that he married his own daughter Abigail to

Elizabeth's brother Dr Thomas Aubrey, Chancellor of St David's. It's a complicated tale of matchmaking across two generations, suggesting that there was life in the old dog, and maybe dynastic ambition… No children, however, came of the union.

It is as difficult to guess at the building and gardening aspirations of Sir Rice as it is those of his father. Sir Rice has not even left any sermons encapsulating his thoughts: his only signature appears on an occasional property deed extant in the archives but not germane to Aberglasney. As someone who caught the eye of James I – and was knighted by Charles I in 1628 – Sir Rice would have frequented courtiers' households and known about their building and gardening projects. Presumably they discussed the royal gardens at Hampton Court, Nonsuch and Wimbledon. They would talk about the gardens made by Sir Thomas Tresham's acquaintances. By 1607 Robert Cecil, Earl of Salisbury, had done a swap with the King and exchanged Theobalds in Hertfordshire for the old Tudor palace at Hatfield. Here he built Hatfield House and laid out new gardens in 1607–1612…

However, this is no place to embark on a survey of early 17th-century garden history. Let us picture the aspiring Rice Rudd at the court of James I and his queen, Anne of Denmark, whose lively patronage of the arts inspired the court masques created by Inigo Jones and Ben Jonson. In the early years of the reign, around 1609, Queen Anne engaged Salomon de Caus to redesign the gardens of Somerset House, her London palace. De Caus, a Huguenot engineer and garden designer, was one of those omni-talented Renaissance men and brought ideas from Italy to his garden-making. He went on to work for Anne at Greenwich and for Henry, Prince of Wales, who held his own court at Richmond until his death in 1612. Inigo Jones, too, came back from visiting Italy newly inspired. There is a tenuous rumour linking him with one William Vaughan of Corsygedol, a Tudor house in North Wales with a gatehouse like Aberglasney's. It is one of those 'It is said' stories that are worth reiterating because someone somewhere may one day find some papers that trace a connection. 'It is said' that Inigo Jones designed the Corsygedol gatehouse. It is dated 1631.

Sir Rice Rudd is, if anything, more elusive than his father. His portrait has disappeared and his signature appears on only a few surviving documents dealing with minor property transactions.

The only numerical or numerological association with Sir Rice is a sinister, almost spooky one: the five maids' deaths presaged by corpse candles, at a time (around 1630) when Sir Rice was engaged in building schemes at Aberglasney. As for other figures – there are the financial losses he incurred in fines for his royalist sympathies during the Civil War, the beginning of the end of the Rudds' fortune. And then there are the 30 hearths recorded in 1670 to reckon Aberglasney's Hearth Tax. Were you to examine the records, you'd find that figure written in a different script from the adjacent entries. Was it changed, or forged?

A handful of plates taken by the photographer C.S. Allen record Aberglasney as it was in about 1870. It had been 'modernized' in the 1840s with various Victorian embellishments. Formal bedding carpets the Cloister Garden, and the corner of the parapet walk in the foreground shows no trace of the hidden entrance.

The Quaint Jacobean Mansion and Garden

No one knows what happened to the Cloister Garden when the Dyers owned and altered the property in the 18th century, apart from a few minor alterations to the northwest corner that have been recorded by archaeologists. The minor changes effected when Thomas Phillips purchased the property around 1803 are also cosmetic. By the end of the 19th century, revivalism of earlier garden styles was all the rage, and a 'Jacobean' garden, possibly original but more often Victorian pastiche, was the height of fashion. Aberglasney followed suit. When the *Gardeners' Chronicle* correspondent visited in 1892, primarily to see the yew tunnel, he was impressed by the 'small but remarkable old piece of gardening close to the house', which he took to be Jacobean. He described the Cloister Garden as having a central fountain, which was unearthed by archaeologists early in the 1990s. He did not mention the pattern of formal bedding, but a corner of it can be glimpsed in the photograph of 1870 and is confirmed by the Ordnance Survey map of 1887. Sometime in that century two Irish yews were planted to add formality and emphasize the central archway leading to the pond garden.

The Victorian fountain means there was a precedent for incorporating a water feature in the restoration. Water was actually channelled in a conduit under the house and across the Cloister Garden before building took place! No sophisticated 17th-century Englishman would have passed up an opportunity for an Italianate display of waterworks.

But all this was on a much higher ground level – tons of soil must have been brought in over the years, augmented by rubble and, more recently, self-composting plant material that buried the fountain. Aberglasney Restoration Trust was determined to get down to base level – to discover, for instance, the true depth of the arches.

Restoration Comedy

Implementing any restoration project involves political manoeuvring akin to a stately pavane. Let's say you want to rebuild a wall.

Having done your homework with the aid of your own experts and advisers, you put your proposal to, say, the Heritage Lottery Fund panel. Their experts and advisers consider its merits. They may query aspects, and you adjust your specifications. This may go on for some time, the 'dancers' regrouping in new positions and going through their choreographed paces once again, with the appropriate courtesies.

Once you have gained approval, you begin to go ahead. However, every time something unexpected crops up (and this happens on an old site) consultation begins again. Where history has been blurred by time, there are usually differences of interpretation and opinion about what should be done. All the while the clock is ticking away, eating up the days and hours before some deadline – such as an official opening ceremony, or a big bank holiday weekend when the public is likely to appear in droves. All the while the

Hidden behind vegetation, the profile of the west façade was barely recognizable as recently as 1998. It is hard for today's visitors to imagine how dilapidated and overgrown the property became before restoration began.

60 Aberglasney

meter is clocking up extra fees for consultants, extra planning time, extra materials. And all this before you finish the work and – in the fullness of time – receive the promised funding for it.

At Aberglasney reconstruction and archaeology have had to proceed hand in hand. The parapet structures around the Cloister Garden, for example, had to be made sound before the area in their lee could be excavated. Periodically, as you repair stonework, new factors emerge. It is only when you come face to face with the task of repointing a wall that has been obscured for years by ivy that you perhaps find a straight line or see a change in the rhythm of the stones that tells you a section of wall has been patched or infilled. The excitement of finding some hidden clue… The attempts to interpret the new findings. The dilemma of whether to stop and excavate. The need to change the plan.

The corner of the parapet walk nearest the front of the house and the entrance is an example. The higher level was reached via a ramp (highly convenient for disabled access, always a consideration for garden owners seeking funding and planning approval). The stonework of this ramp was repaired and finished with its sandstone capping along with the rest of the raised walkway – *before* archaeologists realized that it was a Victorian innovation. Only when the adjacent stonework was exposed for repointing did it become possible to read the scars and seams in the stone and understand that the original builders had made a double flight of steps to the higher level. Beside it, hidden in the thickness of the structure, and infilled with rubble, was a little 'room' excitingly floored with the first glimpse of a patterned paving. The discoveries did not end there.

Opposite, top 'Restoring' the Cloister Garden marks a milestone in the Aberglasney saga: the structures surrounding it are the project's *raison d'être*, yet the treatment of the central space has been largely a matter for informed conjecture. Wide random cobbling flanks the 'outer' ranges to north and south.

Opposite & below, left to right Across the axis leading from the Gatehouse, the diaper-pattern cobbling is being reinstated. The central panels are to be a flower-rich sward, initially grass. As their geometry is pegged out, gardener Peter Gosling points out to Chris Beardshaw some of the adjustments that the plans must make to suit the lie of the land.

Original diaper-patterned
cobbling was uncovered first in
the hidden room and then on
the path to the Gatehouse. The
pattern of sandstone tiles laid
end-on within a framework of
limestone is being re-created
across the Cloister Garden.

The Criss-cross Path

The decorative but practical diaper-patterned cobbling has now become a familiar Aberglasney hallmark. As archaeologists and restoration masons worked hand in hand, the extent of the path that marks the original 'grand approach' to Aberglasney was revealed in three exciting stages.

First came the discovery of the hidden 'room'. Archaeologists don't only peer downwards but look about them, seeking context. The little paved room was in alignment with the archway of the Gatehouse tower. Was there once a through passage? Close examination of the outer surface of the parapet walk suggested it had indeed been walled in at a later date. Sure enough, digging uncovered a patterned walkway leading straight from the Gatehouse to the blocked-in-archway room. But did it go any farther? Beyond the archway into the 'cloistered' enclosure?

The archaeological team by now were trowelling down to basics within the Cloister Garden. The early ground level had been far lower than of late. One way or another tons of soil had accrued in the Cloister Garden, raising its level by feet, and reducing the proportions of the arched embrasures to pygmy dimensions. When these skiploads of soil were scraped away, an 'original' level was established – and there, etched in its surface, were the ghostly impressions – the imprints – of those diaper patterns. The third section of patterned paving to be discovered was the most extraordinary. It wasn't there! The stones had long ago been 'robbed out' for other, unknown uses. The pattern went right across the enclosure, parallel to the house's west façade, to an answering 'room', or archway, which was excavated in the opposite parapet walk. By now Aberglasney had opened its gates to the public. Someone sprinkled sand in the grooves to show how the pattern had run. It was clear that this element had to be restored.

The remainder of the Cloister Garden dig yielded less clear-cut results. Patches of random cobbling running along the side ranges. Evidence of retaining walls marking terraces across the slope, apparently punctuated with flights of steps. Some post-holes. A series of puzzling furrows that looked superficially like ridged-up potato beds, but were incised into subsoil in prime position in the enclosure: eventually an expert came up with the suggestion that they were the basic drainage for planting beds, and would have been covered with topsoil before being planted.

For a year or two the Cloister Garden lay fallow while the final layers were dug away, measurements taken and feasibility studies begun. 'Can we have a water feature?' someone asked. 'Perhaps some rills trickling water down the slope?' 'What about an ornamental parterre?' 'Maybe, but what pattern, and what kind of plants?' To silent music that pavane started up again, its stateliness sometimes veering towards skirmish. Proposals, considerations, counter-suggestions. Because this is the core of the historic site, one may not impose on the space anything that was not known to be there. Thus a water feature or parterre pattern of the period is unacceptable because no evidence exists of what it looked like. Where there were walls and traces of steps, walls and steps must be reinstated – although the flights of steps occur in odd places.

And the centrepiece of this most special of gardens? What in all the wonderful world of plants will we be able to feast our eyes on?

Just as laying a carpet turns a space into a room, so covering bare earth with turf has an instantly civilizing effect on the ground in the Cloister Garden, seen here from the southwest corner of the parapet walk.

From the second storey of the house, above the bay windows, you can see over the western parapet range to the adjoining garden enclosure, formerly the kitchen garden. The noted garden designer Penelope Hobhouse created a sumptuous new planting plan for this area, which had been completely derelict.

Grass. A panel of green grass. It is what the Powers That Be decree. They who must be obeyed.

Graham Rankin, Director of Operations, is a fine plantsman. Here he will turn on its head the usual gardener's pride in the perfect lawn. He will positively encourage *weeds*. Period weeds, of course: daisies (perhaps double ones, or the 'hen-and-chicken' kind – Gerard's 'childing daisie'), fritillaries, violets, little species tulips, crocuses and colchicums, perhaps the odd strawberry. It will look like the flower-embroidered robe of an Elizabethan lady. It will be a flowery mead.

Floor Show

It is always interesting watching the visitors who pause on the raised walkway to look down into the Cloister Garden space. They always wave their hands about and do a lot of pointing, explaining to one another their ideas, or indicating strange discrepancies, such as differing arches. Even visiting garden history experts do it: they too are foxed by the odd shapes, the lack of symmetry, the way the layout doesn't conform to any known type. Perhaps this is something to relish. Who ever said history was simple?

'It requires but little effort on the part of a wanderer in this charming garden of old times to people the place once more with the gentlemen and pretty ladies of Jacobean times.'

Gardeners' Chronicle, 1892

Aberglasney made history by opening to the public before restoration was complete. People who had seen stages of the excavation on television and heard Kevin Blockley's ongoing comments were fascinated to see it in the mud and the flesh. 'Is that Kevin?' they would ask the guides. The sight of archaeologists still scraping away at buried stones offered an added attraction, comparable to watching monkeys grooming each other in a zoo. 'Ooh, look at that one, he's found something!' This might be one solution to the dilemma of How to Treat the Cloister Garden – to leave it forever unfinished, but people it with human specimens, just as landowners once set hermits to inhabit their grottoes. A series of archaeological anchorites (preferably with long dark hair like Kevin's) could endlessly scrape at stones. It could be part of an employment training programme or a work experience module. It might even qualify for grant funding.

ST FAGANS
The Lost Garden of a Musing Soul

It is not difficult to see how the Italian Garden became a hidden garden. What is more of a puzzle is to understand in what sense this hidden garden was thought to be Italian.

In this instance we do know who the garden-makers were – both she for whom the garden was made and the masterly head gardener who saw that the work was done. The latter's name was Hugh Pettigrew, and he was the Kew-trained son of the head gardener of the Marquis of Bute – who, it's said, owned the parts of Cardiff that the Plymouths didn't own. (The benefit of family connections could operate on either side of the green baize door.) As head gardener, Mr Pettigrew ruled the St Fagans roost from 1898 to 1935. His was an extraordinarily powerful position: outdoors a head gardener had authority equivalent to that held by the butler indoors.

Milady comes with a sheaf of appellations to choose from. Her father was Sir Augustus Paget, the British ambassador to Copenhagen, Rome and Vienna. Her mother, born Walburga Hohenthal in a schloss near Leipzig, was a friend of the Princess Royal, Queen Victoria's eldest daughter and wife of Prince Frederick, son of Kaiser Wilhelm I. Alberta Victoria Sarah Caroline Paget was a goddaughter of the Queen. From her childhood she was always known as Gay – not, it seems, an appropriate nickname for the 'very beautiful, very slow and sad' lady who was never known to smile, at least not in paintings or photographs. Her melancholy expression was captured by Edward Burne-Jones in one of his rare society portraits. In 1883, at the age of 18, she married Robert Windsor-Clive, who had inherited the title of 14th Baron Windsor at the age of 12. In 1905 the lapsed Earldom of Plymouth was revived, and she became Lady Plymouth. At St Fagans, thanks to her husband's involvement in local politics, she also found herself, in 1896 and 1905 respectively, the wife of the Lord Mayor of Cardiff and the Lord Lieutenant of Glamorgan.

The cast for the first act of 'The Italian Garden', an intimate period drama of St Fagans, is a small one. It consists of a husband and wife, two mothers-in-law (one already retreating into dowerhood after

An Outline of the Plot...

For the last half of the 20th century St Fagans was the Welsh Folk Museum. Just recently, with 'folk' out of fashion and a wider range of history encompassed, its name was changed to the Museum of Welsh Life. In 1946 the Earl of Plymouth donated the Grade I listed house and 18 acres of land to the National Museum of Wales. Typical examples of historic buildings were dismantled stone by stone from sites all over Wales and re-erected in the grounds. The site has been extended and now covers almost 105 acres.

At the core of St Fagans remains the Castle, a fine Elizabethan manor house built on the site of a Norman motte and bailey, and its pleasure grounds. Begun in 1580, the building was completed in 1620 by Edward and Blanche Lewis. Elizabeth, a Lewis heiress, married the 3rd Earl of Plymouth in 1730. For most of the 18th century the house was tenanted, but in 1850 it was refurbished for the heir to the Plymouth estate. The house was modernized internally and terraced gardens in Victorian style were added.

Our Windsors (or Plymouths), Gay and Robert, spent part of every summer at St Fagans with their three sons and daughter. Under their ownership, the Victorian gardens were restyled in up-to-the-minute Edwardian mode. It is the Italian Garden in this complex that is currently being restored.

The Parterre beside the Castle, once known as the Dutch Garden, is kept bright with seasonal bedding.

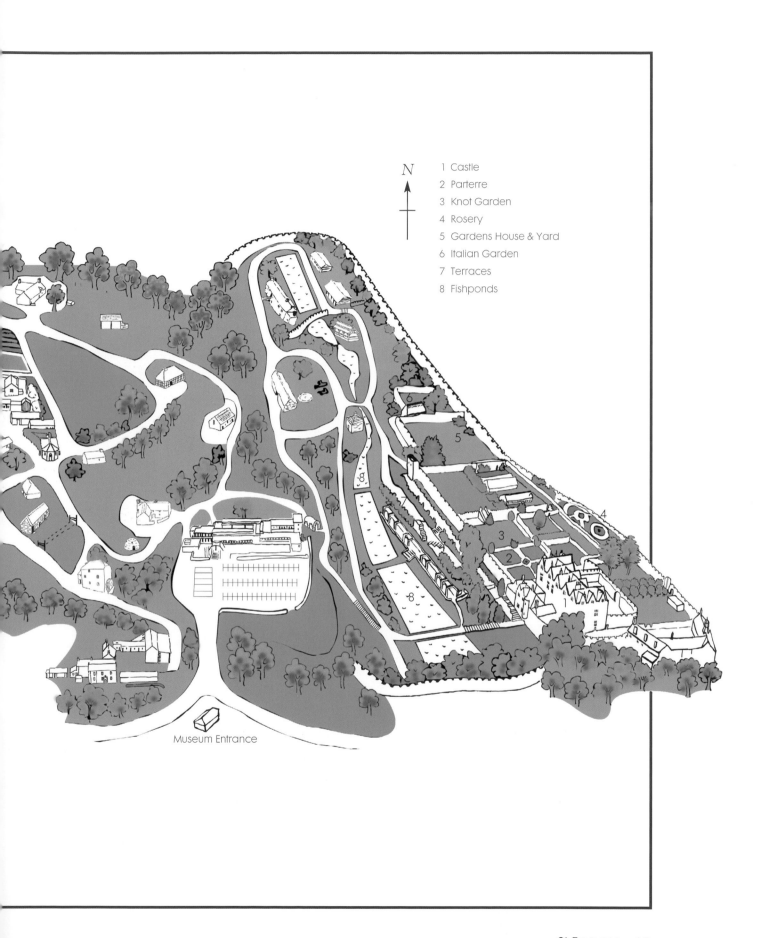

1 Castle
2 Parterre
3 Knot Garden
4 Rosery
5 Gardens House & Yard
6 Italian Garden
7 Terraces
8 Fishponds

Museum Entrance

leaving her mark on the gardens), and the head gardener. They are joined on occasion by children, visitors, retainers and others.

At St Fagans Gay Windsor seems to have epitomized the conscientious lady of the manor and dutiful landowner's wife, especially after her husband's accumulated honours. She had not always moved in such serious society. In her younger days she had fallen in with the exclusive circle known as the Souls. They crystallized as a group in the mid-1880s in the house parties given by Lady Elcho and Mrs William Grenfell (later Lady Desborough) at Stanway and Taplow. Gatherings of the Souls rang with the family names of Wyndham, Charteris, Tennant, Cust, Windsor and Grenfell, and with those of distinguished individuals such as the Prime Minister A.J. Balfour and the statesman Lord Curzon. The coterie shared rather high-minded intellectual and aesthetic tastes, indulged with wit and humour. The women were admired for their social gifts, their loveliness, their sense of fantasy and fun, and their intelligence, which could intimidate outsiders: one of them was dismissed by a potential beau as 'a very nice filly, but she's read too many books for me'. Perhaps the quiet Gay Windsor verged on the more soulful side of the group, but she was certainly a member in her passion for art and music. She had her bedroom at the family's main residence, Hewell Grange, decorated with a frieze of monumental figures intended to symbolize Beethoven's *Pastoral Symphony*.

Gay's mark on the St Fagans interior seems lighter, less monumental. One example suggests the informal aesthetic of the Souls: photographs taken inside the Castle in her day show simple bunches of annuals stuck in a vase or a rustic beer mug in the spirit of the artist Kate Greenaway. (One wonders what became of the blooms from the thousand rose bushes Mr Pettigrew planted to provide cut flowers.)

Gay Windsor's soulful spirit seems to haunt certain parts of the Castle gardens – we imagine her reading poetry in the moated bower of the new Rosery, and generally beautifying the already beautiful setting, fine-tuned in the capable hands of Mr Pettigrew. She represents a still centre of activity, with a scrum of cricketing children and devoted dachshunds as her satellites. There must have been more boisterous moments. We know of her experimenting with bicycles, and swimming in the fishponds during hot summers. Sir John Lavery's painting of 1905 (see opposite) gilds the picture of family life on an Edwardian afternoon. But a sense of Gay's creative will in the making of the

gardens is missing – or can be felt only indirectly. Perhaps the terraces to the west of the Castle, drenched in warm afternoon sun, reflect a taste of Italy with their ornamentation of classical urns, terracotta planters and lead figures in the style of Dutch sculptor Jan van Nost.

Her husband was the enthusiast, and in partnership with Hugh Pettigrew embarked on major gardening schemes. Lord Windsor was a tree freak (a trait he perhaps inherited from his mother, Lady Mary Windsor-Clive). Some of his specimen trees are still on the terraces, and he laid out some 100 acres of parkland to the west of the Castle as woodland criss-crossed by formal rides in a style inspired by the woods around Versailles. The trees are now interspersed with the buildings of the Museum of Welsh Life, and its main car park now occupies the site of the extensive new productive garden laid out under Pettigrew. This relocation of the kitchen garden freed up space near the Castle, where within the existing walled enclosures Pettigrew developed a series of new 'garden rooms' suggesting the influence of William Robinson and the Arts and Crafts gardeners of the time. Borders of exuberant perennials, often colour-themed, or plantings of bright annuals were framed by clipped hedges and panels of grass. His masterpiece was the elaborate new Rosery (a spelling preferred at St Fagans over the now more common 'rosary'), which, as we shall see, had formerly occupied the space that became the Italian Garden.

A Family Group at St Fagans, 1905 was painted by Sir John Lavery in the year that Lord Windsor was created 1st Earl of Plymouth. Lady Windsor's mother, Lady Paget, in the foreground, recorded sitting '...for Mr Lavery, who has got a reputation, is Irish, and adores Whistler. Windsor had this picture painted as a record of himself, his wife and the children. It is a group on a garden terrace...'

You can imagine Lord Windsor actually plunging a fork into the ground to mark where he wanted a particular tree planted. By contrast, Gay comes over not like the down-to-earth Cecily in *The Importance of Being Earnest*, who calls a spade a spade, but more as someone like Gwendolen, who states: 'I am glad to say I have never seen a spade.'

Perhaps we should think of her as an inspiration, or as a rather wonderful garden ornament.

The Italian Influence

The revivalist gardens in formal style that the later Victorians and their Edwardian successors created around houses such as St Fagans often claimed descent from historical precedent. They were variously named Old English, Dutch, French, Italian – the description denoting some supposed characteristic of lay-out, planting, materials or ornament. To us they just tend to look Victorian or Edwardian.

Gay Windsor brought to the Edwardian concept of the Italian garden the sophistication and taste of an elite upbringing, and authentic experience of Italian culture. St Fagans Castle was merely a second home. After their marriage the Windsors had rebuilt Hewell Grange, their Worcestershire seat, at the phenomenal expense of about a quarter of a million pounds. The cost reflected the owners' ambitious ideas on interior decor. The design of the building was based on Montacute House in Somerset, but within it was modelled as a Renaissance palace. Gay's father held diplomatic office in Rome, so the Windsors spent much time in Italy and were able to observe the originals at first hand. The ceiling of one of the rooms at the Grange was copied from the 15th-century d'Este apartments in the Corte Real of the Gonzaga Palace in Mantua. Much of the decoration and furniture

The Knot Garden (above and right) is a modern creation in an old enclosure, in keeping with the ethos of the Castle gardens. The formality of Victorian and Edwardian styles is sympathetic to a house begun in Elizabeth I's reign and refurbished in Victoria's.

was Italianate in style, and the house seemed to Gay's mother to be 'blazing with gorgeous Italian colour'. (How times change. Hewell Grange has now become a detention centre for young offenders.)

An Italian Garden at St Fagans is not likely, then, to have been some off-the-peg design, but the creation of someone steeped in genuine Italian culture, and someone with her own artistic talent, notably for sculpture.

How to Find a Hidden Garden

When Chris Beardshaw decided to seek out Lady Windsor's hidden garden, he was directed to the northernmost of the enclosures that run northwards from the Castle. Here you come up against a series of almost blank walls. They are variously boundary walls separating the gardens from the public road through the village, garden partitions (sometimes brick-lined on the sunny side) and walls supporting buildings on the far side. The Italian Garden is surrounded by some of these high walls, and you could easily not know it was there.

It occupies a narrow, kinked rectangle at the very toe of the tapering wedge of gardens squeezed against the road to the north of the Castle. It is buffered from the gardens that people visit by the more functional enclosure surrounding Gardens House, the Victorian home of head gardeners, on the south side, and by a dense grove of evergreens to the west. At least twice in recent decades it became seriously overgrown and hidden by vegetation, to be cleared once in the late 1970s (about the time the Museum acquired it from the Plymouth Estate) and again in 2001. Seedling sycamores, ivy and other arborial opportunists took advantage of the tiniest gaps in those high walls, the paving, steps and raised pool surround, and their roots prised their way in, making the stonework heave and crack. A lower order of weeds completed the cover-up with a dense blanket of brambles, willow-herb and other aggressive intruders.

The Italian Garden could have been lost in a more permanent way. A handy plot of land like this next to a road might be considered a prime target for development in this fashionably old-fashioned village near Cardiff. The artful developer/planner might squeeze a couple of bijou dwellings into such a space. Or the garden owners, desperate for space, might have turned it into a car park, a canteen, or a home for storage tanks… This could have happened at any time in history until St Fagans became a conservation area. More recently historic gardens like this one have gained some protection by being listed.

In a sense, the Italian Garden was hidden from the first. The *Country Life* issue of 20 September 1902 featured a splendid 12-page jamboree of an article on 'St Fagans Castle, Cardiff, the Seat of Lord Windsor'. It is sumptuously illustrated. Agapanthus bristles on the battlements, pelargoniums tumble from pots. The prose of the anonymous author (later identified as Henry Avray Tipping, architectural writer for the magazine) displays similar exuberance. The walks, terraces, ponds, fountains and lead cistern are depicted in photographs; and so are some of the garden enclosures to the north of the Castle, particularly the 'moated rose garden' and the 'garden of annuals'. No mention of an Italian Garden, regrettably: it would be a treat to read how this enclosure struck the eloquent Mr Tipping. He approved of the lack of 'stiff and formal gardening', praising the free and natural manner in which the borders of hardy flowers were arranged, the panels of annuals framed in greensward ('a delightful example of gay and successful gardening'). He also noted that the old-fashioned orchard was made an enchanting place of beauty by spring bulbs. If the new rose garden was 'a perfect dream of loveliness', would he have found the Italian Garden a place of calm and seclusion? A pool of deep tranquillity? A sun-trap, reminiscent of the warm south? Would he have recognized it as a tribute to Italy if it had been presented to him as 'The Italian Garden'?

Avray Tipping did not mention the Italian Garden because it was still being made – probably at precisely the moment of his visit. Head gardener Hugh Pettigrew's *Handlist of Roses* at St Fagans contains the clue. It also sets the keynote for a resonant

A rare 'autochrome' photograph from the archives is one of a handful that document early 20th-century planting. The unidentified child (perhaps a young Pettigrew?) is dwarfed by the tiered plants in the herbaceous border. Such records offer an inspiration to today's gardeners to replicate the sumptuousness of the effect.

rose theme unifying the Castle gardens, and provides an invitation to explore another splendid recent restoration – the Rosery, complete with moat.

A Language of Roses

Mr Pettigrew compiled his *Handlist* in June 1904. It numbers 68 different rose beds in the Castle grounds, including those in the formal gardens, in hedges separating different areas, on poles and chains on the terraces and between the ponds, and trained on walls. It must have been roses all the way in the pleasure grounds, but backstage, too, roses occupied every available corner. Beds 33 to 46 served as a 'Trial Rosery', and the location of Bed 58a was the 'South Side of Cucumber Pit'. Bed 61 is defined as 'Walls in Italian Garden', and 17 rose varieties are named as growing there. The new kitchen garden contained more than a thousand roses 'for cutting purposes'.

Roses on the Italian Garden Walls

Bouquet d'Or (T.)*
Climbing Marie Van Houtte (T.)
Cheshunt Hybrid (H.T.)
Dr Rouges (T.)
England's Glory (T.)
François Crousse (H.T.)
Gloire de Dijon (T.)
Gaston Chandon (T.)
Homère (T.)
Mrs Paul (B.)
Madame Bérard (T.)
Purity (H.B.)
Rêve d'Or (N.)
Rampant (Ever.)
Turner's Crimson Rambler (Cl. Poly.)
Tea Rambler (T.)
William Allen Richardson (N.)

Gloire de Dijon

Bouquet d'Or

* Hugh Pettigrew's brackets indicate the classification of the time, such as Tea, Hybrid Tea, Noisette, Climbing Polyantha, etc.

William Allen Richardson

So the Italian Garden was in existence in June 1904. Mr Pettigrew gives more helpful information. The Rosery was 'of recent formation' – it had been established in 1899–1900. 'Until then the Rosery occupied the site of what is known now as the Italian Garden, a position too shut in to attain the best result in Rose culture.' Then we have a fuller explanation:

'THE ITALIAN GARDEN. The Roses on the high walls which surround it are mostly those originally planted when it was made into a Rosery over forty years ago. Two years since, when it was made into its new form, with the water tanks and the low wall to retain the terracing, these Roses were left untouched.'

'Two years since' brings us to 1902, the year of the *Country Life* article. Another hundred years and we find the BBC filming the restoration of the Italian Garden. The centenary seems to be a neat coincidence. In the Italian Garden in the first years of the new millennium the only remaining evidence of roses is a series of metal bars driven into the walls (and it takes a hawk-eyed garden detective to find them). These were threaded with wires for the roses to be tied into, like a feint-ruled page waiting to be written on. Picture the wire-ruled walls at the turn of the 19th century, criss-crossed with the stems and blooms of the 17 varieties on Mr Pettigrew's list.

The gardeners are already nurturing half a dozen or more of these varieties, and stockpiling new wires and brackets in readiness for the restoration. Whether they will locate the obscurer names is anybody's guess. But at least they have had some practice in the previous major restoration project.

Reviving the Rosery

The restoration of Pettigrew's Rosery was undertaken as part of the Museum's 50th birthday celebrations, along with renovations to the Castle. It was proposed by estate manager Andrew Dixey, who had long cherished the idea, but he admitted: 'I hadn't imagined it might be undertaken at such speed!' Thus he found himself in the shoes of many a head gardener or estate manager of past times, whose employer rode in and demanded something like a Capability Brown makeover or a new wilderness at the drop of a hat. It was the beginning of a sharp learning curve that has benefited rose culture all over the gardens.

Pettigrew's new Rosery was 'situated opposite the Church of St Fagans, and separated from the rest of the garden by a very old wall'. Roses still grew in the triangular enclosure when Andrew Dixey and his team broached the restoration, but the design had been considerably simplified in the decades after the war, obliterating the original layout. This was complicated in plan, involving a row of three overlapping circles flanked by segmented beds. In the vertical plane it was equally complicated, with an intricate framework of trellises and arches that expanded the display areas upwards and overhead. The rose-covered centrepiece was Lady Windsor's hazelnut arbour, encircled in turn by a bay hedge, a 'sleeping beauty' rustic trellis and a narrow moat or canal lined with terracotta tiles. At one end a trellis segregated the beds of polite bourbons and bush teas from the less orderly hybrid perpetuals and multifloras

'The garden at St Fagans is very much like a dream, too beautiful to be true. Pettigrew, the new young gardener, is full of enthusiasm.'

Walburga, Lady Paget

beyond. The trellis design was copied directly from a drawing printed in *The Formal Garden in England* by Reginald Blomfield and F. Inigo Thomas (1892), which originated as a woodcut in *The Countrie Farm* (1616) by Gervase Markham (itself a translation of C. Estienne and R. Liébault's 16th-century *Maison Rustique*). Here we have an ideal design synthesis in a centuries-old garden – the Elizabethan/Jacobean and the Victorian/Edwardian in perfect harmony as the garden complement to the Elizabethan Castle with its Victorian gloss.

The Rosery restoration team worked from contemporary photographs, the listings and thumbnail plan in Pettigrew's *Handlist*, and a limited amount of experimental garden archaeology. They found some tiles for the canal *in situ*, but were puzzled by their terracotta colouring: in the monochrome *Country Life* photographs the canal looked white. The museum photographer happened along and was able to explain that the photographic process of those times often rendered reds as very light shades. This was another piece in the puzzle, another morsel of knowledge that might be useful sometime in the future. A terracotta-tiled canal was therefore reinstated, along with the other structures.

It only remained to find and replant the original roses. In this quest, Andrew Dixey was often advised 'Don't!' It is notoriously difficult to trace old roses. Some cultivars just fail; others disappear. Old names can sound very similar, were often misspelt or misapplied, and some have been re-used. When you do think you've found a named rose, you can't always be sure it's the one that was grown at St

Once virtually a 'hidden garden', the recently restored Rosery (opposite) is an eloquent success story. Sufficient records remained to re-create the original design of 1899–1900, including the early 17th-century lattice-work frames (below) repopularized by writers in the 1890s.

Fagans. Not even top rosarians can always verify identifications. The quest for old roses would fill a lengthy television series and does fill many books.

There must have been something of the 'twitcher' in Hugh Pettigrew with his exhaustive lists of roses. You can imagine his delight at obtaining some new variety before a rival garden got it. There was certainly an element of keeping up with the Joneses. Roses with local connections included 'Corallina', bred by the Paul nursery for the Cory family of Duffryn House near by, and the 'Mrs Stephen Treseder', bred by the famous Cardiff nursery of Treseder. (Andrew Dixey is still trying to rediscover an authentic specimen of this white tea rose.) On the other hand, Pettigrew was also a pragmatic gardener prepared to experiment and presumably to discard varieties that did not come up to scratch. Hence his Trial Rosery: 'The idea for this Rosery is to use it for limited quantities, or limited new varieties, so as to have them there under close observation to prove their worth and their adaptability, or otherwise, for more extensive culture in the Gardens.' Here lies a hint that there were problems with some of these

'Mme Alfred Carrière' is an elegant, hardy Noisette climber, whose scent, sustained performance and French pedigree made her a favourite among turn-of-the-century gardeners such as Mr Pettigrew.

roses even then. Today Andrew Dixey struggles with mildew and rust, but he remains sanguine about such matters. 'We try to explain to the visitors that these problems help to highlight how conditions have changed over a century' – such as the sulphur-laden atmosphere that could kill people but cure rose disease. He adds, 'The perfume of many of the old roses surely makes growing them worthwhile.'

Pettigrew's Trial Rosery of oblong beds cut out of the turf surrounded by borders was close to the entrance to the Italian Garden. Today, in much the same area, near Gardens House, you will find beds lined up with rose stocks. Here the gardeners use time-honoured techniques to bud the sought-after varieties on to the host plants. The search for budwood goes on not just throughout Britain and in famous European rosaries such as Sangerhausen in Germany, but all over the world. A rose for the St Fagans Rosery called 'Beryl' was traced to California. Other named roses have been located in New Zealand. It's an exciting

moment when a precious packet of budwood arrives, having jetted halfway around the world to be spliced into your stock. Rose experts reckon that the 'Beryl' now growing at St Fagans may well be the first in cultivation in Britain since World War II. ('But,' mutter the gardeners under their breath, with the shade of Mr Pettigrew hovering over them, 'who can say how it will do?')

Roses come and go. Like old varieties of apple, they have often fallen out of cultivation for good reason. They may be especially vulnerable to disease, or have simply been superseded by 'better' cultivars, which often means more commercially viable ones. Ideally, someone somewhere keeps a stock of the old varieties, out of scholarly interest, for reference purposes and to maintain the gene bank.

Some visitors might expect a museum to see itself as a repository of such relics of the past. Gardens, however, are different from humidity-controlled stores where inanimate treasures can be wrapped in acid-free paper and handled with special cotton gloves. Plants are

The climbing habit of 'Mme Alfred Carrière' brings her fragrant blooms conveniently to nose level on the wooden framework of the Rosery. Behind, in trellis-edged beds, the gardeners follow the Victorian practice of pegging down rose stems with forked sticks to encourage a froth of bubbling blooms.

wayward beasts, living and growing and breeding – and catching things – and requiring constant human attention and unlimited expertise. (Mr Pettigrew would be surprised to find how few gardeners are employed on site today, and deeply shocked that they no longer serve a long and gruelling apprenticeship.) On the 'plus' side, in the century since he compiled his list, enormous leaps in rose breeding have put many 'more efficient' rose cultivars on the market. Pettigrew would have leapt at the novelties, planted them in his Trial Beds and allowed them to graduate into the garden if he deemed them garden-worthy. Gardening, like gardens, does not stand still.

Snapshots

The Italian Garden was not taken by that *Country Life* photographer in 1902, and may never have been formally photographed. To find out what it looked like the garden staff at St Fagans have trawled through the archives for glimpses in old photograph albums, and combed memoirs and diaries for allusions. They have asked people what they remember. And they have dug about in the garden itself.

In the late 1970s Hugh Pettigrew's son, Andrew, was asked to draw a plan of the garden enclosure as he remembered it. The resulting sketch plan is a beautifully accurate outline of the plot, yielding useful information and posing a few dilemmas. His colouring shows the planting in the beds as multicoloured. (Such planting is ephemeral, so the restoration team may have another agenda.) He shows the pool as pale blue. (Blue? Oh, dear. Decidedly suburban these days. Even if it was once blue, does the re-created pool have to be blue? Call in the forensics experts and paint detectives to check on this.)

Half a dozen old photographs have come to light with a setting that can be clearly identified as the Italian Garden, once you get your eye in. From them you can glimpse the sort of details that would otherwise be lost – the style of the seats and of the different planters (if not always the plants they contain), and whether the pool was planted and so on. The World War I photograph (opposite) of nurses and medical orderlies posing in a sunny corner near French windows shows wooden seats and clipped evergreens, possibly orange trees, in Versailles

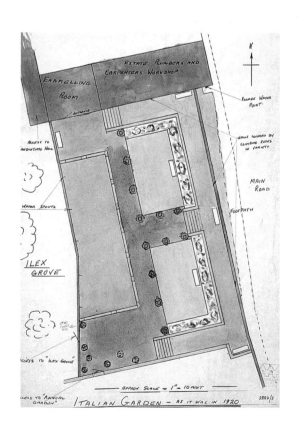

The head gardener's son, Andrew Pettigrew, made this sketch of the Italian Garden as he remembered it in its heyday. The kink in the western wall dates from the time when this garden was part of the village and lay outside the Castle precincts.

cases. (Some of these would overwinter in that corner studio space with the French windows.) The pool looks clear of plants, and around its margins are oblong planters filled with what looks like summer bedding (pansies, perhaps) in the foreground. These elucidate a detail in Andrew Pettigrew's sketch that might otherwise be overlooked. Eleven little oblongs are drawn on the pool surround, presumably relating to the positioning of these planters.

The trouble with garden seats is that in photographs they are often obscured by people sitting on them. However, enough is visible of what the forgotten people are posing on to confirm that this is the standard issue St Fagans seat, found in other parts of the gardens, and readily replicated for the Italian Garden restoration. Two or three archive snaps of anonymous young ladies in their Sunday best tell us that the seats were flanked with tubs of agapanthus. Behind them we see that the east wall in the background was covered in trained roses. The roses form the backdrop to a commemorative photo of serried ranks of dressed-up children standing on the central steps so they could all be fitted into the picture. The image is imperfect because the glass plate has been broken, but it adds its shreds of evidence to

A grainy snapshot of nurses and orderlies posing outside the Enamelling Room shows that the Italian Garden was being beautifully maintained during World War I. At this point the pool appears to be clear of planting.

the garden jigsaw. Another snapshot from a different angle shows a young lady holding a bunch of flowers. Who she is interests the garden sleuth less than the fact that spiky water plants like irises are clearly growing in the pool behind her. We'd really like to identify them.

There are similarly oblique glimpses of the Italian Garden in the vivid memoirs of the indomitable Walburga, Lady Paget. They show that two years after it was made it had become just another garden. By 1903 the small room in the northwest corner had been fitted out as a garden room-cum-studio and had become known as the Enamelling Room. Here Lady Paget could escape bad weather, and even the grandchildren to whom she was devoted. ('It did not *rain*, but sheets of water descended as out of buckets. I did not mind it so much, as I spent my whole time enamelling in the ideal room Gay has had arranged for it. Enamelling is a most engrossing occupation; also in this wet weather, the burning stove gives a delightful feeling of comfort on a chilly August day.')

The family seems to have spent some time at St Fagans between July and September each year. 'The month at St Fagans passed like a dream,' Lady Paget wrote in 1904. That year she worked at her enamelling, making 'two great candelabra with about 360 pieces of enamel' that were to be encased in silver on her next visit. Another year she made a looking glass 'with enamelled flowers all over it'. So much time did she spend in her 'workshop' that she once confided, 'When I die I shall probably haunt that place.' No home should be without such a haven for a mother-in-law, even if it does mean her shade returning.

In Mind of Italy

Deborah Evans is Senior Garden Conservator of the National Museum of Wales. Gerallt Nash is Curator, Historic Buildings and Commerce. (Their titles fit the context, as we're in a museum: elsewhere we find custodian, director, gardener…) Together with estate manager Andrew Dixey, armed with the existing evidence, the team should find little difficulty in restoring the hard landscaping and the planting. Apart, that is, from the 'challenge' of repairing the dilapidated walls and damaged cut-stone paving; of designing grass steps stout enough to withstand the feet of visitors; of laying on a new water source with circulating pump (the old reservoir supply being long gone); and of locating the original rose cultivars listed by Mr Pettigrew.

Meanwhile, for the TV series Chris Beardshaw and the BBC researchers are keen to explore parallels for the Italian aspect of the story. Could the film crew fly to Italy and shoot the original garden that provided the inspiration for this one? No such place. Could they visit other Victorian or Edwardian gardens in Britain that would make a telling comparison? This is where students of landscape architecture display their historical expertise, and Chris and Deborah pore over lists of turn-of-the-century gardens with Italian influence. One by one they are crossed off the list. St Fagans doesn't fit any pattern. An Italian garden should display some degree of symmetry. Instead of the

The 19th-century terraces with their architectural treatment have an Italianate, if not Italian, atmosphere. In the Plymouths' day they looked out over Versailles-style woodlands, today studded with the buildings of the Museum of Welsh Life, relocated from all over the country.

Above Restoring the Italian Garden involves serious hard landscaping. Cleared for action, the dereliction contrasts tellingly with the scene in the World War I photograph on page 85.

Opposite The Enamelling Room, pool surround and raised walk call for rebuilding, while substantial seedling trees have to be extracted from high up in the Gardens Yard wall.

enamelling-room-cum-orangery tucked into the corner, you'd expect some kind of more formal loggia, perhaps accessible from the house, or an orthodox garden building, marking a more decisive and interesting transition between indoors and out. You might also expect the water feature to consist either of a sunken pool, with water surface at ground level, or of a fountain of greater character than the large, featureless raised tank that occupies a substantial proportion of the St Fagans garden area.

Deborah Evans interprets the Italian influence here as being mutated through the Arts and Crafts gardening ideas that characterize the other gardens of Pettigrew's day rather than deriving from more architecturally rigorous Victorian Italianate traditions. The raised water and raised grass walk make the main ground level seem more like a Lutyens/Jekyll sunken garden. The cut-stone paving unique to the formal gardens at St Fagans is decidedly un-Italian. (Here we should perhaps relate the tradition that the other mother-in-law, Lady Mary Windsor-Clive, used to trace out with a chalk-tipped stick the serpentine outlines she sought to pave her paths. Stonemasons would cut out the jigsaw shapes accordingly. It was one way of giving employment to the artisan.)

What does feel Italian about the spot is a grove of evergreen oak (*Quercus ilex*) and cypress just beyond the walls to the west, before the open ground falls steeply to the pools. There is a cork oak further down the slope. To enter the deep shade of the Ilex Grove on a sunny day (and particularly from the unusually warm walled enclosure) must have been to experience precisely the kind of acute sensual contrast you get in Mediterranean climates. The Windsors had first met in Rome. Perhaps as they wandered through the former Rosery they were wont to say to one another, 'Doesn't this remind you of Italy?' while Mr Pettigrew more prosaically described the enclosure as 'a position too shut in to attain the best in Rose culture'. Pettigrew too had visited Europe, having apparently worked for the Rothschild family near Geneva in the early 1890s, and perhaps knew what Continental summers could be like. But here he was wearing his head gardener's hat and was concerned about mildew and lack of air circulation on the health of his roses.

It is worth noting that the summer of 1899 was particularly hot. 'The heat at St Fagans was great and enchanting. We had all meals out of doors... Such a summer had not been known in this century. The earth's heat was 75°, the flowers were all burnt up and even the shrubs began to suffer... Gay and the children bathed in the fishponds every morning.' Fishponds were not to Lady Paget's taste: she preferred the 'rushing streams over beds of gravel' of her childhood in Germany.

Lord Windsor and Mr Pettigrew expanded the pleasure grounds with terracing to the north and west of the Italian garden between 1903 and 1906. A concrete-lined swimming pool was installed on the lower terrace, although the weather never again made the water so tempting as it was in 1899.

Blue Is the Colour...

The swimming-pool interior decor is not recorded (it now serves as the feed pool for the Museum's woollen mill). We have played through the first act of the Italian Garden drama, and wait in the wings to see how its sequel, the restoration, proceeds. In the programme notes, perhaps, we record in the interval that neither fishponds nor concrete swimming pool were considered safe for the children of Robert and Gay's successor, the 2nd Earl. They used the tank in the Italian Garden, presumably supervised by a nanny who kept the dry towels ready in the Enamelling Room. At some point the waterplants had been taken out, the tank drained and cleaned, and repainted – in suburban swimming-pool blue.

Beneath the scraps of blue paint that still adhere in places to the concrete, our forensic experts discover an earlier layer of colour. This proves to be a dark shade of grey – the sombre, neutral lining that makes a water feature a reflecting pool, mirroring the changing skies and creating its own living, mutating coloration. Thank goodness!

The blue element could perhaps be represented in living colour in the summer borders below the raised grass walk. Chris Beardshaw could no doubt suggest a breathtaking plant list. With the tubs of agapanthus as a keynote, think anchusa, campanula, delphinium, eryngium, veronica, geranium, larkspur, polemonium, scabious, salvia... Think Mediterranean-sky blue.

Watch this space as it comes back to life, and see if it makes you think of Italy.

With lead figures in the style of van Nost, the St Fagans terraces have a distinct echo of those at Powis Castle, 75 miles to the north. Perhaps the Windsor-Clives were influenced by their Herbert cousins in their 19th-century rebuilding of the terraces.

HIDCOTE
The Mystery of the Missing Lists

'What on earth could be hidden at Hidcote?'

The question has become familiar to Chris Beardshaw as he and the camera crew head for the Cotswolds and for Major Lawrence Johnston's garden at Hidcote Bartrim – probably one of the most famous and most photographed gardens in Britain. Many thousands of visitors each year explore it and see nothing missing. How can this be a 'hidden garden'? 'Well,' answers head gardener Glyn Jones, 'one way or another, it's a matter of lost plants...'

'Where's my peacock?' asked former gardener Jack Percival, eyeing a rampant box tree. In Johnston's day it was one of the neat topiary forms, bought ready-made, that were one of the extravagances of the garden in its earliest years.

Somewhere in that tangle of box branches lurks the peacock, waiting to be cut free. It's the best part of a century since Major Johnston began his garden, and over 50 years since the National Trust took it over. Inevitably, some parts of the garden become overgrown, with precious plants and other treasures crowded out by more vigorous neighbours. For a while 'low-maintenance' ground-cover planting was favoured over the high-upkeep perennials and tender plants of a plantsman's garden, and this helped to eclipse the original picture. You will sometimes see Glyn setting forth armed with saw, loppers, pruners and matching steely glint in his eye.

But there's another way in which plants have to be rediscovered. Everyone knows Lawrence Johnston was a consummate plantsman, but no one has been sure just what he planted where. Apparently, he made no plant lists, drew up no planting plans or blueprints for the garden layout. Nor, when they acquired the garden, did the National Trust make an inventory of the plants or garden features and ornaments (though they did of the contents of the house). Whether other records have disappeared, been destroyed or didn't exist is a case for the detectives – National Trust detectives, in this instance.

After Johnston died, ornaments from the garden were dispersed, and his library of 500 books was sold for £7. In these days of heritage

An Outline of the Plot...

The pioneering garden created by Lawrence Johnston at Hidcote is world-famous. The hallmark of the great English gardens of the early 20th century is strong structure married to inspired plantsmanship. Hidcote was made by an Anglicized American brought up in Europe.

In 1907 the widowed Mrs Gertrude Winthrop bought for her son the hamlet of Hidcote Bartrim in Gloucestershire. It comprised a farmhouse, farm buildings and cottages, and 300 acres of land, plus a handsome cedar of Lebanon, a few beech trees and a small, partly walled kitchen garden. On this site Johnston created his masterpiece. He laid out garden rooms near the house, created further formal gardens around two main axes – along the Stilt Garden with its pavilions and the Long Walk – and then planted up the more informal areas of the Stream Garden and Westonbirt. All the time he was filling the garden with fine plants, often new discoveries, and steadily gaining recognition and acclaim.

Frozen leaves in winter.

For some years Johnston spent his winters on the French Riviera. In 1948 he handed Hidcote over to the National Trust before retiring permanently to La Serre de la Madone, where he died in 1958.

Hidcote was also pioneering in that it was the first property acquired by the National Trust for the sake of its garden rather than for the architectural quality of its building. Hidcote was 'where the Trust learned to garden', and all admit this was a steep learning curve. As it approaches its centenary, this much-visited garden, Grade I-listed since 1984, is undergoing a series of facelifts. Much of the original planting is being reinstated, and other alterations are in hand to allow the visitor to experience the garden more as it was in Lawrence Johnston's day.

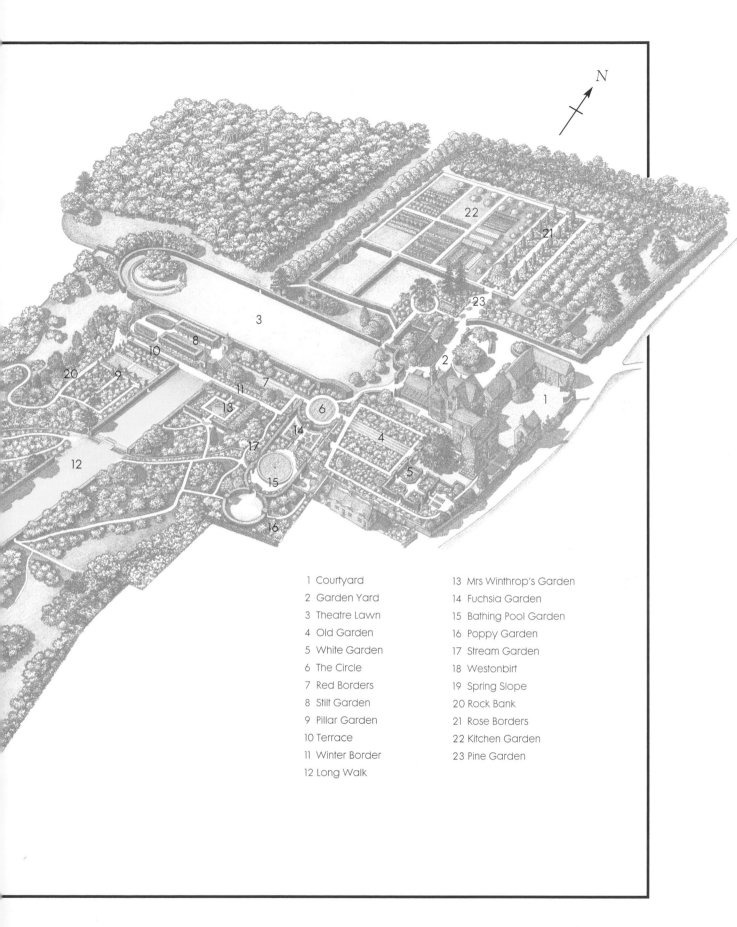

1 Courtyard
2 Garden Yard
3 Theatre Lawn
4 Old Garden
5 White Garden
6 The Circle
7 Red Borders
8 Stilt Garden
9 Pillar Garden
10 Terrace
11 Winter Border
12 Long Walk

13 Mrs Winthrop's Garden
14 Fuchsia Garden
15 Bathing Pool Garden
16 Poppy Garden
17 Stream Garden
18 Westonbirt
19 Spring Slope
20 Rock Bank
21 Rose Borders
22 Kitchen Garden
23 Pine Garden

Seen here beyond the wall of
the Old Garden, the house at
Hidcote ('more cottage than
manor – Cotswold and
domestically charming')
is curiously peripheral to the
layout of the gardens.

The cedar of Lebanon, planted 'too near the house for comfort', is one of the few garden landmarks that date from before 1907, when Mrs Winthrop bought Hidcote for her son, Lawrence Johnston.

and conservation, to lose this kind of inheritance seems unfortunate, if not careless. But consider how times have changed. Today the gardens of the National Trust are national treasures. Hidcote now makes money for the Trust, but in the early years of post-war Britain it was a serious financial and administrative liability. No one knew quite how to set about running a garden. The Trust's learning curve in dealing with Hidcote marked the first faltering steps in an amazing journey that put new worlds of garden visiting on the map.

Hidcote is also a victim of that success. With garden visiting a national pastime, managing wear and tear on paths and lawns becomes a major problem in any popular property. Some of Johnston's garden buildings were notoriously flimsy, and his hard landscaping cheaply done: the shelters where he overwintered tender plants collapsed years ago, and the friable Cotswold stone he used for his paths and bridges has already reached its 'best-before' date and is gradually being replaced. It's not just the fabric of a garden that suffers. An architectural layout like Hidcote's, with rooms and corridors packed with plant interest, suffers from 'pinch-points', professional jargon for places that cause bottlenecks in visitor circulation. The whole *raison d'être* of a compartmented, structured garden is its invitation for you to explore its secrets (preferably alone, or in ideal company – certainly not in a crowd).

Johnston made his garden in three broad brush-strokes. He enlarged the house and laid out a series of formal garden 'rooms' in its lee before the outbreak of World War I. Despite wartime restrictions and his own active service, he managed to extend the main axis through the Red Borders to the Stilt Garden with its pavilions, establishing bolder lines and more classical, architectural plantings. From about 1920 he added two further masterstrokes – the Theatre Lawn and the beginning of the Long Walk – as well as the Pillar Garden. By the mid-1920s he had extended the Long Walk and created Westonbirt.

You first encounter Hidcote in pictures, out there, at arm's length, two-dimensional and flat on the page or screen. You go to the place and find yourself lured in and enclosed, not claustrophobically, but by the gentle skill of a master. You feel the peace of one pro-portioned space, and then are drawn to explore another, glimpsed through some opening… As you get to know Hidcote better, you find there are changes of level between the different garden enclosures, as the garden paces out the contours of the site. You realize you have to make another visit, beginning your exploration anew from a different point. And all this before you even start to think about the detail of all those plants.

In 1950, the garden opened three afternoons a week and visitors totalled 3500 a year. Johnston complained that they spoilt 'the pleasure of a garden which should be a place of repose and to get away from the world'. In 2001 nearly 140,000 visits were recorded.

A Harvest of Words

The phenomenon that is Hidcote elicits varied responses, ranging from silent admiration to exclamations of pleasure. Some four generations

Above The gateway from the Old Garden frames a vista along the garden's first strong axis – across the Circle, along the Red Borders and through the Stilt Garden.

Right The earliest area Johnston designed consists of the series of intimate garden rooms opening from one another. Box-edged beds in the Fuchsia Garden are blue with scillas in spring before the fuchsias are planted out. Beyond, the Bathing Pool Garden is flanked by yew architecture – topiary birds and a Palladian portico.

of eminent garden writers have flocked to the place to describe its intricacies, trace its influences and express their impressions. If verbiage were foliage, Hidcote would never run short of leaf-mould. Even a guidebook must deal not just with the development of the garden and the 28 garden areas listed on the plan, but with the fourth dimension of their symphonic performance in spring, summer and autumn. Paradoxically, the literature compounds the problem of visitor pressure: not only does everyone want to see Hidcote, but they want to see it repeatedly, as it changes through the seasons. It's a self-perpetuating problem. Soon everyone will be planning further visits to see the results of the current refurbishment.

One of the rare photographs of Lawrence Johnston, pictured on the Theatre Lawn towards the end of his time at Hidcote. His little pack of dachshunds helped him in his hunting pursuits. (Earlier he kept spaniels for the same purpose.)

Equally eminent plantsmen have surveyed and recorded the planting at various times. A plant catalogue runs to many, many syllables, and there are numerous plant lists. And all this is not counting any descriptions and lists that have been lost, such as Johnston's correspondence with plantsmen of the Royal Botanic Gardens at Kew, or plant notes that have been destroyed. Careful sleuthing among articles, letters and lists of plants for sale at Hidcote, and scrutiny of old photographs, have come up with a host of plant names.

Even more words were generated behind the scenes as the National Trust began to explore the challenge of bringing Hidcote into a new century, and reviving some of the fine planting that made the garden a touchstone in Johnston's day. Historian Katie Fretwell and her colleagues combed the literature for useful comments and pertinent descriptions, consulted everyone who could be consulted, trawled through unfathomed archive material and perused all available plant lists. Her splendid 'Survey 1999–2000' provides a *catalogue raisonné* of all known sources, and brings to light some revealing new material.

Johnston's own article about his not very successful plant-hunting expedition to Kilimanjaro in 1928 comes across as an exercise in self-promotion, the presence of the author eclipsing the subject of plants (which, admittedly, were disappointing on that occasion). Perhaps, though, this gives us a glimpse of the egotism that so irritated his co-plant-hunters. A new-found letter from George Forrest expresses this with splenetic eloquence. Also entertaining – but an editor's nightmare – is a draft article about Hidcote in pullulating purple prose by Nancy Lindsay, a kind of self-appointed protégée/protector of Johnston. The inconveniently ardent lady, who could 'empty a ballroom in 15 minutes' (according to her cousin Lady Diana Cooper), has much the same effect on the page – the reader retreats exhausted after a couple of image-saturated sentences. Her enthusiasm is admirable (a school report might say), but she should not try so hard.

Hidcote's Hidden Maker

For all that has been written about his garden, Lawrence Johnston remains one of Hidcote's most elusive secrets. He was a shy, retiring man who hated being photographed and who seems to have left no diaries and little correspondence. Whether he ever kept detailed

The Theatre Lawn today, with young beech trees on the dais replacing lost originals. Like the Long Walk, this expansive green space is a touch of genius, offering relief (if any were needed) from the incident-packed garden rooms with attention-grabbing planting. As always, the view gives a hint of something beyond to explore: here an ogee roof behind the hedge.

records of his garden planting remains a matter of debate. He made precise notes on plant-hunting trips, and some commentators are convinced that he and his gardeners would have kept meticulous garden records. Some evidence has clearly been lost over the years. On the other hand, even if there were lists, it may be that there never were planting plans for Hidcote. In laying out his garden, Johnston was more a canes-and-string man than a graph-paper plotter. His genius allowed him to create a geometry that works for the eye, although the angles are not right, and to adjust levels so that the awkward fall of the ground becomes an advantage. Somewhere in his peripatetic upbringing in Europe and the USA, Lawrence Johnston had observed and absorbed the architectural models that turned his natural artistic talent into a genius for garden-making. Exactly where this came from is a mystery. 'He has the best natural taste of anyone I ever knew,' commented Arthur Bateman, an architect from nearby Broadway. A potted biography reveals little. Descriptions and remarks about the man range from the adulatory (usually from plant enthusiasts) to scathing (from those who did not share this passion, or were rubbed up the wrong way).

Beneath the quiet exterior lurked great intensity. It shows in the sensualist who painted in oils as well as with plants, and in the player who fought ferocious bouts on the tennis court. He was both fastidious and thorough, perhaps reflecting his cavalry training. He fought with honours in the Boer War, and was twice wounded in action in World War I. (During periods of convalescence he managed some of the most dramatic developments in his Hidcote garden…) Occasionally his biography rises to melodramatic heights. He was left for dead after the battle of Hooge Château until Colonel Henry Sidney, an old friend from Broadway, noticed some movement and rescued him. The dominant mother makes another interesting theme.

Lawrence Waterbury Johnston was born in 1871 in France to wealthy American parents, spent a great deal of his youth in Europe, and became a naturalized British citizen. By 1898, Gertrude Winthrop, Lawrence Johnston's mother, had lost two rich husbands, a daughter and a second son. 'Lawrie' had been a sickly child, perhaps

'Highly eclectic, Hidcote presents very compactly an original synthesis of historic and contemporary gardens.'

Russell Page

The ogee roof seen from the Theatre Lawn belongs to one of a pair of 'small and highly fantastic' pavilions between the Red Borders and the Stilt Garden, created by Johnston around 1914. The North Pavilion is a small room decorated with Delft tiles. Johnston's interior decoration in deep, warm colours reflecting the adjacent Red Borders has recently been re-created.

explaining the possessive mother theme. In 1907 she purchased
Hidcote for her son. It was conveniently close to the town of
Broadway, a centre for Arts and Crafts gardening activity, and honey-
pot to expatriate Americans. She seemed to think her son 'a wanton
spendthrift', holding the purse strings even after her death by

The North Pavilion's twin is effectively a portico, with double glass doors framing a foreshortened view down the Long Walk.

bequeathing her capital to distant cousins and leaving Lawrie only the interest. Comments by James Lees-Milne are waspish and dismissive: 'a dull little man... Mother-ridden. Mrs Winthrop, swathed in grey satin from neck to ankle, would never let him out of her sight.'

Johnston was snobbish about people as well as plants, not exerting himself in company unless impassioned by discussing plants and gardens with other members of the gardening élite. His neighbours on the French Riviera were crème de la crème types, socially and horti-culturally. One of them was the American writer and gardener Edith

Wharton, and it's tempting to picture Johnston as one of her characters, or someone out of a Henry James novel.

No Smoke without Fire

Among the *Who's Who* of Johnston's gardening friends was Norah Lindsay, 'plantswoman, garden designer and society butterfly' – and, like Gay Windsor of St Fagans, one of the circle that called themselves the Souls. According to the landscape architect Russell Page, the herbaceous planting in her garden at Sutton Courtenay had 'an air of rapture and spontaneity' and may well have influenced Johnston's approach. Norah's daughter Nancy credited her with inspiring his interest in old roses. Nancy Lindsay lacked her mother's social graces but gradually became very close to 'Johnny'. It was to Nancy that, since he had no relatives, he bequeathed La Serre de la Madone, his French property. (She promptly sold up, after donating important plant material to the Cambridge Botanic Gardens.)

Two teasing pieces of gossip attach themselves to Nancy. The first, that she was Johnston's illegitimate daughter, can be dismissed outright as ridiculous. It is valuable only in that it illuminates how incomprehensible in the eyes of the world was this attachment between the dry, introverted man 'old enough to be her father' and the eccentric, effusive younger woman. If the man on the Clapham omnibus finds this hard to understand, the bond is clear to any plant enthusiast: these were two ardent plantspeople whose common interest spanned the generation gap. Nancy was a passionate plantswoman and an intrepid plant-hunter, exploring remote parts of Turkestan and the Near East alone in the belief that 'if she travelled with a man they would both almost certainly have been killed, but as a solitary woman she was safe'. The image-charged prose in her draft article about Hidcote is indigestible precisely because of the extraordinary sensuality with which she strives to describe the plants she loves: '[Peony] "Aurora" flouts the dawn with candid waterlilies of pink cornelian and lustrous leaves of celadon. "Perle Rose" has foliage irised as a pigeon's breast aquamarine and hyacinth, ruby and olivine and imperial flowers of pink mother-of-pearl...' And so on for pages.

The second rumour about Nancy has more credence. She became rather a thorn in the flesh of the people who took over the management

In the reverse of the scene shown opposite, the South Pavilion becomes an eye-catcher at the end of the Long Walk. The streamlet that crosses the grassy vista is visible in this uphill view, whereas from the higher level of the pavilion it is hidden in the undulating ground, in the same way that a ha-ha is concealed from the key viewpoint.

The Red Borders created in 1910–14 are colour-themed mixtures of shrubs, perennials, bulbs and annuals, perhaps reflecting Johnston's painterly training (red meaning anything from orange to maroon) rather than contemporary fashion theories. Originally they provided colour primarily in late summer, but today the season begins earlier, with massed tulips.

of Hidcote when Johnston passed it to the National Trust and retired to France. This was an entirely novel situation for all concerned, and there were many teething problems during the negotiations and the early years of managing the garden. Proprietorial about her relationship with 'Johnny', Nancy Lindsay offered herself as guardian. 'My position is that of a very old and devoted friend of Johnny's who knows Hidcote as well as he does himself… I know his plans for every yard of it,' she wrote to Lord Esher, Chairman of the Trust. After many unwanted overtures on her part, Jack Rathbone, Secretary of the Trust, finally told her she was *persona non grata* on the local garden committee. Her response sounded stoical: 'I've never thanked you for your charming letter!!!!', she wrote to Rathbone, providing a list of rose names and adding that she hoped to keep in touch. Her actions were less commendable. 'She was seen to make a bonfire of the garden records in the yard, and this is probably when Johnston's planting books, etc. were lost.'

Explorers and Gentlemen

Lawrence Johnston didn't simply subscribe to the plant-hunting expeditions that many of his contemporaries sponsored. He went plant-hunting himself – at first only in Europe. Mrs Winthrop died in 1926. Once released from her apron strings, Lawrence set off further afield. Picture the Major in 1927 exploring South Africa and what was then Tanganyika. His companions included Captain Collingwood (Cherry) Ingram, Reginald Cory collecting plants to embellish his Mawson garden at Duffryn, George Taylor, later director of Kew – and, for his personal comfort and convenience, his own uniformed chauffeur/valet and cook. (To Cherry Ingram this seemed 'a bit of an extravaganza'.) Johnston made another trip to Kilimanjaro in 1928, the one he recorded in his *New Flora and Sylva* article that year as 'disappointing'.

Many hybrids between typical red and yellow forms of *Paeonia delavayi* occur in the wild. Botanists have given them a host of names but most have been 'lumped' by Chinese taxonomists into the single species *P. delavayi*. The name comes from Père Delavay, one of the French missionaries who collected so many new plants in China in the late 19th century that the Paris natural history museum took years to sort them out.

In 1931 Lawrence Johnston set off plant-hunting again. This time it was with the veteran plant-collector George Forrest on the last of his seven fruitful trips to various parts of western China, Tibet and upper Burma. The pair planned an ambitious year-long expedition to collect in Burma and Yunnan. This time there was no chauffeur and valet, but a beleaguered Forrest left to do all the work while the Major gadded about 'riding in the morning, tea and tennis in the afternoons and bridge at the club in the evening'.

Partnership with Johnston brought the seasoned Forrest to his knees. 'Had I raked G.B. with a small tooth comb I couldn't have found a worse companion than Johnston,' he wrote. Johnston treated Forrest as if he was 'a Cook's courier arranging a tour for him', leaving him to engage chairs and chair-bearers, coolies and mule transport, and to organize stores while he had fun. He also took irresponsible health risks in the primitive conditions up-country, given that he suffered from malaria and had only one lung. After Johnston caught a severe chill 'through exhausting himself in playing tennis and then sitting cooling off instead of changing', Forrest set off alone across the border to Tengyueh (now Tengchong) only to find Johnston arriving a few days later against all medical advice. He fell ill again and finally consented to return home (Forrest devoutly hoped – 'but he changes his mind more frequently than his socks'), pausing only for a final quibble about payment of his share of the stores for the trip. 'Johnston is not a man, not even a bachelor, but a right good old Spinster spoilt by being born male. A person more selfish I have yet to meet…'

This was Forrest's last trip. He died of a heart attack at the end of the expedition, but some significant plants nevertheless came back from it, including the white-flowered *Jasminum polyanthum* and two mahonias. *Mahonia lomariifolia*, with long, shapely leaves, still grows in the shelter of the courtyard at Hidcote. Its more tender relative *M. siamensis* was planted in Johnston's garden on the Riviera.

Return of the Tree Ferns

Replanting is an ongoing task at Hidcote. Visitors were intrigued on a July day in 2001 to witness a scrummage between more or less equal numbers of gardeners and tree ferns in an area near the Pillar Garden. Much discussion was going on about exactly where the dicksonias

Hidcote is famous for its hedges, grown from a wide spectrum of plant material, to provide 'high walls for sky-roofed rooms'. They tease the visitor by offering inviting glimpses of further garden spaces, while creating microclimates to shelter plants from searing winds. (Low 'keep-off-the-grass' railings are a reminder of the wear and tear that visitors entail.)

Glyn Jones discusses the tree ferns with Chris Beardshaw (right). The five permanently planted specimens of *Dicksonia antarctica* have their crowns protected from frosts by wigs of straw, until new fronds looking like crosiers (below) uncurl in spring. The gardeners remove the specimens of the more tender *D. australis* to greenhouse shelter to overwinter.

were to be positioned. It was a puzzling sight. Hidcote didn't seem to be at all the place you could expect to find these 'modern' gardening icons, apparently being planted into bare earth. Plantsmen know they need deep, acid woodland soil and shelter: in their native Australia they form an understorey to the high canopy of eucalyptus forests. Plant snobbery deplores their proliferation in designer gardens and dictates that they look at home in ravines, not high on the Cotswold plateau. Seasoned garden visitors know they thrive and even multiply in Cornwall, southern Ireland and western Scotland, areas where the Gulf Stream gives humid, sheltered gardens subtropical luxuriance. Had Hidcote suddenly succumbed to garden-centre fashion planting? Was this an instant make-over?

Naturally not. Hidcote was being true to itself. When former gardener Jack Percival revisited the garden in the late 1990s one of his questions was: 'What's happened to the tree ferns? Mr Johnston had tree ferns here.' He indicated a corner to the east of Mrs Winthrop's Garden, where the geometry of the garden rooms just begins to melt into the informality of the Stream Garden. Here a thuggish cotoneaster had swamped everything in its shadow. 'We had tree peonies here, too,'

Mr Percival added. Any tree ferns were long gone, but when the cotoneaster was removed the gardeners discovered one of the original tree peonies, a survivor of this long-lived genus.

Replacement planting was put on the agenda. Tree ferns are serious instant make-over plants. (They did look rather surprised and self-conscious in the bare soil that July day, without the companion blechnums and the herbaceous plants that now lap at their feet.) You don't 'plant' a tree fern in the conventional way by teasing out a root ball, making sure the roots are well surrounded by soil and then waiting for branches, leaves and so on to grow. You order a plant (resembling a stick) of the size you want, make a hole deep enough to keep it upright and stick it in. Given sufficient moisture, roots will regenerate and fronds appear. The 'trunk' – actually numerous layers of fibrous root or caudex – grows only an inch or so a year, and the price is reckoned by the foot. A fern 3 feet high might easily be 50 years old and cost about £100.

'Perhaps his most important contribution to modern gardening was his ability to combine plants in an unusual way.'

Russell Page

In recent years the unusual growth habit and relative rarity of tree ferns has led to an illicit trade in the plants, so now they may be officially removed from Australia only by those who have been granted special extraction licences. Those sold outside their native habitat have 'passports' to show that they have been legally imported from approved areas. Nonetheless, European Customs officers are frequently confiscating contraband cargoes. Originally, some are supposed to have arrived as ships' ballast, looking more like hairy logs than living plants, and then surprising people by sprouting fronds. Specimens from the batch received by the famous Treseder nursery at Truro in the 1880s still flourish in Cornish gardens today.

Lawrence Johnston's choice of tree ferns and his success in growing them at Hidcote demonstrate his gardening strategies. This shady, sheltered spot is at the heart of the garden, where the winds that tree ferns hate are filtered out by successive barriers of hedging. Johnston remedied the problem of the alkaline Cotswold soil by importing vast amounts of sawdust for the camellias, rhododendrons and other lime-hating plants he wished to grow. The superlative naturalism of his planting was the result of immense calculation and effort.

Pillars and Peonies

Chris Beardshaw and the BBC team are following the reworking of the Pillar Garden as a case study in the current replanting strategy. It's a rectangle tucked into the corner of the 'T' formed by the Stilt Garden and the Long Walk, with the sloping ground graded into shallow terraces. Johnston created it around 1923 as part of his second phase of developing the gardens at Hidcote. It takes up the formal Mediterranean theme of Mrs Winthrop's Garden, which also slopes towards the south and is sheltered by hedges. In Italian gardens columnar cypresses provide upright evergreen punctuation. Here the pillars are of yew, elongated domes permanently anchored on solid cubic blocks, while around and below them ephemeral flowers play their seasonal part, and passing generations tinker with the whole planting scheme. In Johnston's original scheme the yews were echoed by tall poles up which roses grew, and the upright spires of the Japanese cherry *Prunus* 'Amanogawa'. In a *Country Life* article of 1930, H. Avray Tipping noted an abundance of phlox, new and old varieties of rose, and peonies, including 'L'Esperance'. An accompanying

Top and above Regular maintenance, such as clipping and weeding, is routine, but sometimes more radical adjustment is needed.

photograph shows the herbaceous peonies, the glory of the garden in May, tumbling on to the path.

The garden was replanted in 1966 and has had a succession of different herbaceous planting schemes since then. Sometime in the intervening years the phlox had succumbed to eelworm, some of the flowering cherries had been replaced by hawthorns of upright habit (*Crataegus oxyacantha* 'Erectus') and the roses had disappeared. At some point the peonies were planted further back from the path, presumably out of harm's way from visitors. They remain in this position, while behind them other elements of the original garden are being restored, including shrub and climbing roses, phlox and the cherries. New posts like telegraph poles wait to receive and transmit messages between the two climbing roses planted at their feet (plus a clematis planted on the shady side). Glyn Jones almost weeps with rage as he inspects the rose bushes in April: muntjac deer have nibbled the choicest new shoots. Shoot them is what Lawrence Johnston would have done without hesitation. 'Shoot,' calls John Trefor to the BBC team, as the camera focuses on Chris Beardshaw examining the damage. A close-up shot compensates for the fact that the garden is still

Newly planted (each with two climbing roses and a clematis), the 'telegraph poles' of the Pillar Garden will continue to look naked and unadorned until the fledgling climbers are ready to reach for the skies.

pretty stark and raw in its first spring after replanting. It will take a year or two to mature, and the TV series can't wait.

Replacing the tree peonies here and among the tree ferns is a pretext for another plant story. Records tell that among those growing in the Pillar Garden were the yellow 'Souvenir de Maxime Cornu' and 'Chromatella', 'Mme Louis Henri' and *Paeonia suffruticosa* 'Joseph Rock' (also known as 'Rock's Variety', and correctly *P. rockii*). Tree peonies are no more trees than tree ferns are trees: they are woody-stemmed shrubs (*suffruticosa* means having a woody base). The first ones came to England from China in the year of the French Revolution (1789), and plant-hunter Robert Fortune brought a couple of dozen more in the 1840s. You didn't exactly have to

Opulent clumps of herbaceous peonies include delicate pink 'Avant Garde' (above). Nancy Lindsay would have praised its 'elegant chalices'. The tree peony species *Paeonia rockii* (right) is characterized by dark-blotched white petals. Some fine cultivars newly imported from China are being planted at Hidcote.

hunt for them. The Chinese, as usual, had been hybridizing them for centuries: an illustrated book about them was written over a thousand years ago.

The peony named after the American plant-collector Joseph Rock has large single flowers, white with a purple basal blotch on each petal. It's one of several tree peonies that have been replanted at Hidcote. Some of the new ones are plants imported from China, which re-opened its export market in the 1990s. This has made all sorts of wonderful new cultivars available to the West: Johnston would have liked that. The new *Paeonia rockii* varieties have wonderful Chinese names that would have given Nancy Lindsay a whole new world of imagery – the early white 'Bing Shan Xue Lian', the pale pink 'Fen He' and 'Hong Lian' types, and the darker pink 'Shu Sheng Peng Mo'. Here they are, contributing to Hidcote's own private cultural revolution.

Maintenance of hard landscaping is endless. Marrying the cottage ethos of the original design (which was in fact often jerry-built) with the incidental pressures imposed by thousands of feet is a huge challenge to the National Trust. Here hand-baked bricks, hand-cut to shape, are being laid in Mrs Winthrop's Garden in anticipation of the Easter rush.

Another revolution is swinging into motion at Hidcote. Ever since the National Trust acquired the property and began to 'learn to garden', the house has been let to a succession of tenants. All these years the visiting public has entered the garden through the back door or 'tradesman's entrance', via the courtyard and garden yard, to encounter visitor facilities, such as the restaurant and shop, that have grown in a piecemeal way, accommodated wherever there was space around the fringes of the house. Now these necessities no longer accommodate the many visitors, and – what is more important – can distract from the visitors' direct appreciation of the garden. Today, among the plans to make a garden visit more peaceful and fulfilling, are ambitious projects to resite some of these facilities so that they don't impinge on the house or on garden spaces.

Johnston's invited guests would have entered the garden from the house. So, in due course, would it not be fitting if visitors might see the view of the garden from Johnston's study, and, like his guests, approach the garden through the house? They would come out on to the Cedar Lawn and immediately become aware of the long axis towards the Stilt Garden, as well as of the inviting intimacy of the neighbouring garden 'rooms'. To be realistic, in the garden-visiting era of the early 21st century, several hundred thousand pairs of human feet cannot be allowed to compact the soil in which the historic cedar grows: it would be to kill the goose that laid the golden egg. A newly refined compromise has to be made so that Lawrence Johnston's garden remains faithful to his spirit but still accessible to a public seduced by 50 years of publicity. The National Trust is hot on the case, and will find a solution. As a one-time novice gardener, the Trust has certainly come of age.

Above Gardeners work throughout the winter, refurbishing the planting as well as preparing the paths for the next onslaught of visitors.

Opposite Spring in the Pillar Garden sees bare earth hidden under seas of alliums and peonies, and bare supports gradually clothed with clematis tendrils and climbing roses.

THE GIBBERD GARDEN
Restoring an Artist's Vision

Most gardens have a name. This one is properly known as Marsh Lane. But the highway signs around Old Harlow direct you via Marsh Lane to 'The Gibberd Garden' – the equivalent of being directed to St Paul's as 'The Wren Cathedral'. This calls for some ulterior knowledge. It implies something special about the garden-maker, and hints at the way the garden has been named – *after* him rather than *by* him.

Most garden visits begin with your being handed a plan of the garden and a plant list (or, as at Hidcote, a numbered plan of the garden areas). Here you get the plan of the garden, but the small print that looks like a key to the plants turns out to be a numbered list of several dozen artworks. It is tempting to talk about a sculpture garden, but that is the worst thing you can do. There are sculptures and ornaments and there are plants; there are paths and pools, buildings, a stream, grass, trees, sky. It is a garden. But you may not arrive here with such an innocent outlook. You may already know too much.

This is a garden to experience, if you can, as if you were a child. Forget the preconceptions – that it is a Modernist garden, the creation of a man of great artistic vision and the subject of much aesthetic comment. Forget that you have come here in some spirit of reverence because it was made by a Great Man, or because it is on some recommended tour. Don't look for a programmed route around the garden. Suspend disbelief; suspend belief, even. Explore. If you are lucky it will bring out the child in you.

If you forget what you know, you will find wonder in all sorts of shapes. The bole of a tree or the bony knobbliness of a flint may become as intriguing as a rusting metal sculpture or a lichen-encrusted piece of chiselled stone or cast concrete (objects that may happen to be itemized on that list). Sculptors are, after all, very often inspired by organic forms. Anyway, outdoors, in a garden, artefacts are vulnerable to the weathering of the elements in a way that they are not when presented and protected in galleries. They tend to go back to nature. (The pale swan that should surely gleam subtly at the end of the Lime Walk

An Outline of the Plot...

Sir Frederick Gibberd (1908–84) was appointed master planner for Harlow New Town in 1946. His other architectural and landscaping projects include Heathrow Airport, Liverpool Roman Catholic Cathedral, Regent's Park Mosque and the Kielder Reservoir. At Marsh Lane in Essex he put his design principles to work to create something entirely for his own pleasure. The result is acclaimed as one of the few outstanding gardens created in the late 20th century and a rare example of Modernism.

Set amid arable farmland in the Stort valley east of Old Harlow, the site slopes downwards from Marsh Lane and the house to the Pincey Brook on the northern boundary. Sir Frederick acquired the 16-acre smallholding in 1956, inheriting the pool, gazebo and fine lime avenue. (Paradoxically the planner par excellence was denied planning permission to rebuild the 1907 bungalow, and had to settle for alterations.) Sir Frederick expanded the planting, working with nature and the natural topography to create screening masses of woody plants and interrelated spaces – glades, groves and alleys. From the 1970s the garden was 'planted' with the Gibberds' growing collection of modern sculpture and sometimes quirky ornaments. There were corners for playful items, such as a moated castle. Sir Frederick clearly had fun – sometimes with the concrete for which the Modernists are infamous.

The garden's 'cellular' structure was a deliberate exercise in the art of concealment – inviting visitors to explore and discover, while forming a coherent entity. As Sir Frederick consulted the 'genius of the place', the garden grew organically. He relished the way garden designers, unlike architects, could never consider their work finished: 'With us the maintenance period goes on for ever.'

Given Grade II listed status in 1995, the garden is now owned by the Gibberd Garden Trust, formed to realize Sir Frederick's wish that his garden should be open to the public for study and recreation.

Detail of the wire pavilion surrounding the figure of 'Woman with Kid'.

1 Entrance Lawn
2 West Patio
3 Fountain Garden
4 Tapestry Hedge
5 Pool
6 Gazebo
7 Lime Avenue
8 Nut Walk
9 West Paddock
10 Watermeadows
11 Wild Garden
12 Pool and Waterfall
13 Castle & Moat ,
14 East Paddock

N

The House

Marsh Lane

Pincey Brook

0   20 m
66 ft

Sir Frederick Gibberd (1908–84). Lichen and ivy show the effects of time on this concrete cast by Gerda Rubinstein. A bronze cast of the head stands in the Walled Garden to the southwest of the house.

Opposite Robert Koenig's totems, weathering like the wood they are made from, stand among trees fringing the West Vista.

has become camouflaged in the dull subfusc of lichen and time. It no longer draws the eye as the focus of this lofty space. Mightn't Sir Frederick have done something about it?)

Every so often the flints erupt of their own accord from the earth, and each is a wonder in its own right, with a story to tell as arresting as that of Sculptor A or B who moulded clay or iron into this pot or that shape. To the proverbial child, especially one who comes from non-flint country, each is a wonder. The child we would like to be in the Gibberd Garden would be in the happy position of walking closer to the earth than most of us grown-ups, so would notice such things.

We can't escape the concept of the Great Man, the garden-maker, as we explore his garden. Maybe we should regard (and welcome) his own thoughts and the comments of garden historians as footnotes. It's often helpful to read the small print when one's ready. In consulting the 'genius of the place', Gibberd came to know about the flints. They belong to the soil. The family used to collect them from the fields round about. He often used them to bridge the gulf between the ground and the ideas that human incumbents like him imposed upon it – to make paths and platforms for sculpture and to mould contours. He used pebbles to line the stream in the Wild Garden. His predecessors, who must have had some inkling of the same spirit, used small pebbles from the site in the aggregate for the gazebo they built. In these ways the man-made is rooted in its home ground.

The child we would like to be in this garden would also lack the scoring habit of the plant 'twitcher', who seeks only labels (mercifully absent here) and who anyway can't help naming plants. Perhaps those of us who do know about plants should similarly learn to forget. Instead of identifying a flowering cherry, a fastigiate yew, or a clump of bamboo, we should first register them as shapes and enjoy the way they help to articulate the space.

But apart from details of flints and branches and birdsong, our ideal child-visitor would be inspired to make a voyage of discovery of the wider garden – the contrast between exploring a leafy swishing jungle and emerging into a sunny space; the glimpse from behind a screen of bushes of some mystery you'd like to understand better, the gleam of water, the flurry of wildlife… This is to tune in again to the

genius of the place. Sir Frederick spent the first year clearing away the scrub and getting to know the lie of the land that became his garden. He had already done this in the larger landscape, getting a feel for the undulating horizons of the Essex countryside in preparing his plans for the New Town, which was to have a cellular structure relating to the contours of the site. It is no coincidence that the Pincey Brook that bounds the Marsh Lane garden also marked the northern boundary of the New Town.

'It is a garden all about spaces with different materials so that you know you are going from one type of space into another because of the change from grass to paving or to a concrete path.'

Sir Frederick Gibberd

Sir Frederick described his garden as 'a honeycomb sequence of spaces', where the visitor was drawn from one area to another by glimpses of places that enticed them to explore, to discover a variety of enclosures and vistas, areas calling for detailed attention and long, restful views. In this description and in the experience of a visit, there are strong parallels with Hidcote (see pages 92–116). However, the cellular structure at Hidcote, at least in the garden 'rooms', is formal, geometric, symmetrical – components come in pairs or sets that match; Marsh Lane's structure is asymmetrical – based on pairs and groups that balance.

Is This a Hidden Garden?

Signposts notwithstanding, Marsh Lane is something of a secret garden. Not a lot of people know about it. It has been written about and campaigned about, but it is a personal garden. It retains a privacy and remains a mystery to much of the garden-visiting public at large.

It is hidden in the Essex landscape in a way that its maker presumably intended. After leaving Gilden Way, the eponymous Marsh Lane zigzags for half a mile between arable fields (fragrant and fluorescent with oilseed rape in spring), keeping the visitor in suspense. Just as at Clynfyw (see pages 144–166), there is time to wonder if you are on the right track. Eventually you approach the denser mass of taller vegetation that marks the garden, glimpse walls and buildings, and encounter Gerda Rubinstein's fierce guardian eagles perched on the gateposts that reassuringly confirm your arrival (or indicate that you have indeed 'arrived at a more sophisticated environment'). The garden-visiting routine clicks into action, with the entrance payment, the plan of the layout, and the prospect of tea.

Sir Frederick Gibberd used to open his garden to the public in aid of local charities, and enjoyed showing visitors around. He had wished that his garden should eventually pass to the Harlow District Council for the recreation and education of its inhabitants. As it happened, both house and garden had to be sold, but the Gibberd Garden Trust managed to buy them back in order to fulfil Sir Frederick's intentions. The garden was 'saved' thanks to generous donations, fundraising by members of the Trust committee and the Friends of the Garden, and by a grant from the Heritage Lottery Fund. Further donations from individuals and charitable trusts have provided the wherewithal for educational school visits. The Lottery Fund contributed substantially to the appointment of Jean Farley as Restoration Gardener. However, the Gibberd Garden still has to generate income for its upkeep. Jean and another professional gardener, Brian Taylor, work full time at Marsh Lane, helped by several volunteer gardeners, some of whose expertise is formidable: they range from a retired head gardener to specialist plantspeople and part-time horticultural students. The gardeners' task can be a tricky one. They are caught on the horns of the familiar dilemma: 'The garden used to look like that, but now it looks like this. What's to be done?'

The West Vista in late autumn (opposite), with Jean Farley and Chris Beardshaw, and in the spring (above). Sir Frederick saw the vista as a 'river of grass flowing down into the valley'.

This garden is not strictly 'hidden' or 'lost'; it remains visible, but its focus has become blurred, naturally, over time. Landscape design, said Sir Frederick, was the hardest profession because it involved living plants; you had not only to deal with different light each day, but each season was different and you also had to consider growth over the years. 'Planting is fluid and in many dimensions; it's no good planting for the day, if in 10 years' time it's all going to be out of scale.' Almost 20 years after Sir Frederick's death in 1984, the restoration team's impossible task is to try to put themselves in Sir Frederick's place and make the decisions he might have made, act as he might have done. It goes beyond a brief to maintain the status quo, since a garden is a dynamic entity. Another 'fluid' aspect is weather and longer-term climate. The 1970s saw drought years. In the 1990s, too, all the gardening pundits wrote about water shortages and drought-resistant planting styles, while members of the Gibberd Garden Trust referred in the past tense to the wetness of the water-meadows. The first two winters of the new millennium saw the lower parts of the garden under water for weeks on end. Some of the shrubs in the wilderness garden are seriously unhappy because of the waterlogging at their roots, and remedial measures are under discussion. Plans have to be fluid.

Above. The old quince tree has as its companion an unglazed stoneware pot by Monica Young. Tree and pot are naturally shapely focal points.

Opposite The West Patio has a narrow canal set in York stone paving, in which one of Raef Baldwin's upstanding copper fountains watches like a heron.

In his lecture to the Landscape Institute in 1981 Sir Frederick showed a slide of the painting by Sir William Nicholson (in the Tate Gallery) of Gertrude Jekyll's boots – to remind architects that 'we garden designers cannot pack up after the final account and forget all our designs. With us the maintenance period goes on for ever.' But so does the creativity. Remember how, after the shock of losing thousands of majestic trees in the 1987 storm, many gardeners welcomed the opportunity for replanting? Renewal is a part of all gardening. What to renew is another question.

Vision via Television

Various aids (as we have seen in other chapters) are available to the garden 'restorer', from archaeology, dry archival accounts, records and

documentation (some not so dry, as Sir Thomas Tresham's letters showed – see page 27), to visual evidence from maps, paintings and photographs. With the Gibberd Garden we move firmly into the late 20th century. Not only did the garden-maker write and lecture on his ideas and take numerous 'before' and 'after' photographs, but he is recorded for posterity on film, describing the creation and development of his garden. A video is a new way for restorers to learn something about a garden's past. (The attention-shunning Lawrence Johnston of Hidcote, of whom hardly a photograph exists, wouldn't have liked the medium at all.)

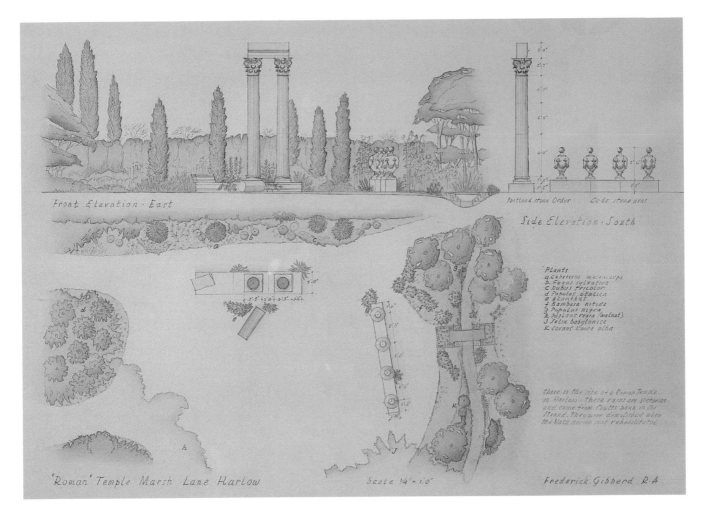

Front Elevation · East

Portland stone Order   Coade stone urns

Side Elevation · South

Plants
a. Cupressus macrocarpa
b. Fagus sylvatica
c. Rubus fricator
d. Populus italica
e. Acanthus
f. Bambusa nitida
g. Populus nigra
h. Juglans regia (walnut)
j. Salix babylonica
k. Cornus kousa alba

there is the site of a Roman Temple
in Harlow. These ruins are pictures
and come from Coutts bank in the
Strand. They were demolished when
the Bath design was rehabilitated.

'Roman' Temple Marsh Lane Harlow   Scale ¼"=1'0"   Frederick Gibberd R.A.

In 1982 Roger Last, himself a fine gardener, filmed an *Omnibus* pro-gramme, introduced by a youthful Barry Norman. Three gardens from *The Englishman's Garden* (1982) by Alvilde Lees-Milne and Rosemary Verey were featured. Marsh Lane was splendidly sandwiched between the Old School, Langford, Oxfordshire – the tailored 'garden room' in Cotswold-stone-vernacular formality belonging to Hardy Amies – and Abbots Ripton, where Lord de Ramsey had the full stately home panoply, from 400-foot herbaceous borders to folly-studded pleasure grounds and landscaped lakes. The programme was a fine trio of contrasts, with Sir Frederick's 'new', modern and personal garden sitting refreshingly between these variations on conventional themes.

Two aspects make this kind of documentation especially valuable. There is the commentary of the garden-maker himself – each of the trio waxed eloquent about his design ideas – and a touch of philoso-phy, each ending with a thought about his garden's future. Then there's the visual record, and a vivid chance to make then-and-now

When Sir Frederick remodelled Coutts bank he bought several fragments of the original façade. He assembled the Corinthian columns and urns in a glade in the West Paddock (opposite), planting acanthus at their feet. With tongue in cheek, he pre-pared a series of architectural drawings of various features in his garden for the 1981 Royal Academy Summer Exhibition, including this one of the 'Roman Temple, Marsh Lane, Harlow' (above). The drawing shows a low skyline punctuated by cypress-like trees in the background.

comparisons. The BBC's *Hidden Gardens* team does a film-within-a-film trick and shows Chris Beardshaw and Jean Farley watching the *Omnibus* programme about the garden together. During the time she has worked here, Jean has come to know the garden well. Some vistas are perfectly recognizable. Other parts of the garden have altered almost beyond recognition. The sculptures provide invaluable reference points in marking the passage of time. Their size (if not always their appearance) remains constant, while the proportions of adjacent planting and surrounding space are subject to change.

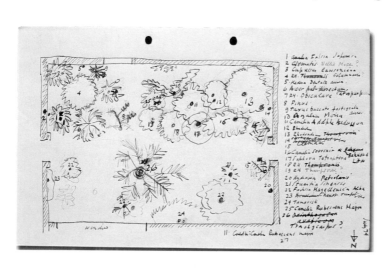

Sir Frederick did not plan his planting on paper, but placed his plants using an intuitive grasp of mass and space. However, he later made a series of sketches to record the planting in different areas – here, the Walled Garden.

Twenty years is a long time in gardening – long enough for a fast-growing tree, such as a birch or poplar, to mature; long enough for many shrubs to get past their best and need replacing, for tree canopies to thicken and exclude light from planting below, for rampant ivy or vigorous flowering climbers to swamp a host tree. Certainly long enough for the spatial relationships of a garden to alter substantially. In the years since Sir Frederick died in 1984 the proportions of much of his planting around the house have altered. Some of the vistas, too, have narrowed or been blurred.

In a lecture to the Landscape Institute he explained how he planned his planting to accommodate adjusting the relative proportions of space and plant mass. He used as an example the blue cedar planted with a laburnum and an almond near the Entrance Lawn. He intended the cedar to become a specimen tree: 'When it is larger the other trees will be felled and the lawn extended – the design adjusted to suit change over time.' But it's not just a question of adjusting what's there. A living gardener travels, gets new ideas, encounters new plants, tires of old ones. It is tempting to add 'is influenced by fashion', but that is not appropriate for Sir Frederick. He would have *made* fashion. (He might have invented decking – concrete decking, maybe.) Inevitably he'd have encountered new plants and visited new gardens – and changed his mind.

Opposite The Ambulatory that once defined the left-hand margin of this space on the West Patio has disappeared. It retains the structure of a garden room, furnished with sculptures and plants.

An element of evolution may prompt alterations. When his children were young the formal pool on the garden's main axis was converted into a swimming-pool. When, to his great relief, the children grew beyond

the swimming-pool stage, Sir Frederick set to work, and in no time at all had a 'garden pool' complete with small fountain, irises, water-lilies, fish and decoy ducks.

Like his friend the architect Clough Williams-Ellis of Portmeirion and Plas Brondanw in North Wales, he liked to 'rescue' artefacts and place them in a witty context. (If Williams-Ellis could have found a place and rescued the dismantled London Bridge, he would have.) Sir Frederick might well have come across further irresistible pieces of architectural salvage and wanted to create somewhere for them, as he did with the columns and urns retrieved when he redesigned Coutts Bank in The Strand. With these he created the impromptu 'Roman ruin' in his Marsh Lane garden. (Harlow was a Roman settlement, he pointed out.) He planted acanthus around the base to echo the foliage of the Corinthian capitals. There was one perfect view of the composition. Sir Frederick was careful not to site the columns in front of any tall trees so that their scale was not diminished but enlarged – an optical illusion no longer maintained now that the planting in the background has matured. Should the restorers take to the chainsaws? What would Sir Frederick have done?

The building of the moated castle in 1981 came about in something of a similar way – partly in response to an abundance of logs sawn from diseased elms, partly after seeing the 'castle' built by Sir Gordon Russell in his Chipping Campden garden. At any rate, there were grandchildren to use as an excuse (if any were needed) for a grandfather to build a solid castle of fantasy. A digger was called in to excavate the moat and pile up the spoil into a mound. The elm logs were up-ended in concentric circles (eventually they were replaced by concrete ones). The whole thing was finished off with a genuine draw-bridge and a flagpole, and made a splendid lookout. It also served a visual purpose: it terminated the secondary long vista from the house.

The view across the formal pool towards the house shows
Sir Frederick's manipulation of the levels by means of terracing. This kind
of landscaping has become commonplace, but it was innovatory in the 1960s.
The swan sculpture by Elisabeth Frink on an oversize plinth is on loan
from Harlow New Town, where its permanent
site is being refurbished.

The moated castle, built of
logs from felled elms, dates
from 1981.

The Art of Space

It could be said that Marsh Lane does have its own 'hidden garden'.
This is the garden as seen from the house, a vital part of the garden
experience conceived by Sir Frederick, but something accessible today
only if you are privileged to be the guest of Lady Patricia Gibberd.
Although her husband was prevented from rebuilding, he made
dramatic changes to the original bungalow, notably creating a lofty
living room with large windows. He created gardens or vistas for each
of the windows.

The Gibberds inherited the apron of horizontal formality to the north of the house, leading to the Lime Avenue. Sir Frederick described the sequence from the house to the garden's margins as passing from architecture through garden to landscape. Paved terraces surround the house and link the pool and gazebo into one architectural composition, extending the formal geometry of the house into the landscape. In country gardens you often find the right-angled patterns of the house echoed in its immediate vicinity, and the lines and the planting gradually softening to blend into the surrounding countryside. It is the details of the way Sir Frederick adjusted the levels formally with a series of stepped terraces, or 'naturally' with slopes and planting behind the tapestry hedge to the west, and with a grotto treatment to the east, that is intriguing. The abrupt change in levels is most clearly observed in the two-storey octagonal gazebo that nestles into the higher ground. Sir Frederick's predilection for concrete textured by exposing the aggregate was anticipated by a predecessor at Marsh Lane, John Blackshaw, who, with his daughters, built the gazebo from sand and gravel dug from the site. They moulded the columns using empty paint tins – surely a piece of improvisation that Sir Frederick would have appreciated. For the original thatched roof he substituted one made of concrete.

Describing the West Vista, Sir Frederick said: 'the sky is the ceiling and the floor a river of grass flowing down into the valley'. The smooth lawn near the house grades into rougher grass in the wilder parts of the garden, unifying the whole. The new living-room window framed the view to the taller trees in the distance (planted in the 1950s) into a beautifully composed picture. However, when you are outside and walking through the area marvellous things happen. Two cast bronze dogs by Robert Clatworthy scamper back towards the house with the happy air of returning from a fulfilling exploration of the depths of the garden (and probably of the Pincey Brook). If, as you walk in the opposite direction, you glimpse just one of them through a gap in the screen of planting, by a trick of relative motion it seems to be the dog that is passing the gap, not you. When you have experienced this effect, it is pleasing to find that this is exactly what Sir Frederick intended: 'Walking around them, they appear to move,' he said.

The East Paddock garden area – between the central axis and the (invisible) functional rectangles formed by the vegetable garden and

The two-storey gazebo is 'rooted' to the change in level by a retaining wall of flints and bottle-glass – 'the bottles put air into the wall instead of concrete and they reflect the light'. The gazebo forms an ivy-clad grotto graced with a terracotta bust of the young Queen Victoria.

the hornbeam-hedged tennis court that now serves as a car park – is more loosely structured. From the formal lawn in front of the house the vista passes over the old orchard to the water-meadow, where the distant castle is the focus. Having shaped the other parts of the site to his satisfaction, a garden-maker might well be tempted to turn his attention to explore the further 'capabilities' of these parts of the grounds. Indeed, Sir Frederick had already drawn up a plan to turn the tennis court into a labyrinth. He intended the raised pattern to be made of hard landscaping – 'there not being time for hedges'. Perhaps in this scheme he would not have insisted on mixing his own concrete, as he usually did, but he would no doubt have specified the constituents and supervised the process attentively.

The Sculpture Element

Though we mustn't call it a sculpture garden, curiosity demands some kind of footnote on this aspect of the garden. Sir Frederick and Lady Gibberd had both been founder members of Harlow Art Trust. They

Opposite, top Gerda Rubinstein's bas-relief tondo on the south face of the gazebo is an affectionate portrait of Sir Frederick at his drawing-board and his wife Patricia engaged in the satisfying pursuit of weeding.

Opposite, below Robert Clatworthy's eager bronze dogs bound homeward, invigorating the West Vista and offering visitors a demonstration of the way spaces come alive as you move through them.

Right Raef Baldwin's fountain in a cone, made from copper pipe and sheet, has acquired a patina of verdigris.

collected works of art, often from young artists who later became well known. In the *Omnibus* interview Sir Frederick explained how each sculpture was integrated into the garden. Generally, it was a case of

'Woman with Kid', once sited beneath the gazebo, is sheltered now by a wire pavilion.

seeing a piece they liked and finding a position for it – perhaps 'planting' a sculpture as you might a newly acquired tree or shrub, in the 'right place'. Occasionally, the setting came first, and a sculpture was found, or commissioned, to inhabit the garden feature. To aficionados the Gibberds' collection of contemporary sculpture represents a fascinating reflection of the culture of the time. To casual garden visitors the varied art forms simply add an extra quality to a very interesting garden. Several of the urns and pots have a domestic quality that harmonizes with the atmosphere of the garden as someone's home, with its productive fruit trees. An unglazed stoneware pot by Monica Young acts as a focal point in the vista, but also serves as a companion to a handsome spreading quince tree partway down the West Paddock. Sir Frederick linked the pot to the living tree by means of a floor pattern of graded flints and stones.

The Nut Walk, near the Quince Tree Vista, was also designed to be seen from the open ground of the West Paddock. Sir Frederick felt that the vista called for a pale statue to bring it to life – ideally in white marble. He commissioned Gerda Rubinstein to create a sculpture for the space. She made the tall white fibreglass figure known as 'Lucinda', the light in the name signalling her role. Sir Frederick described her as perfectly related to that space, the two being completely complementary to each other.

On a visit to Marsh Lane one day, Henry Moore remarked that the pillared ground-floor space of the gazebo reminded him of the setting of a Florentine painting of the Madonna and child. Declaring himself unsympathetic to the concept of virgin birth, Sir Frederick nonetheless liked the conceit and found a different version of gentle feminine care in a sculpture by Fred Kormis – 'Woman with Kid'. (A caprice? The object of the affection is a kid of the animal kind.) The piece now sits in a delicate wire pavilion in a screened space off the West Vista.

The Fountain Garden was a rare example of a sculpture being 'responsible for the garden' around it. Sir Frederick made a new space to make a home for a newly acquired piece – the stainless steel fountain by Antanas Brazdys. Lady Gibberd remembers Sir Frederick working one weekend in 1965, clearing the nettles and reshaping the ground into a shallow bowl and making a circular pool in the centre. 'He did it by eye, instinctively – no measuring or calculation. He had an innate sense of space…' The airy, grassy space was screened and enclosed by shrubby planting. It is brought to life by liquid light playing on the water and the steel.

Working with Nature

It takes a talented and knowledgeable gardener to manage a garden like Marsh Lane so that planting and design stay in partnership. In the *Omnibus* programme Sir Frederick distinguished between the art of garden design and the craft of garden-making-cum-horticulture, where people are so obsessed with plants that they fail to see the whole. They (and, indeed, most garden visitors) tend to notice 'things' and ignore the spaces that enable us to see them. The designer constantly weighs and manipulates the importance of space in that balance. It's something of a paradox in the craft of gardening that formal gardens are 'easier' to maintain than informal ones. Clipping hedges and shaped bushes to the designated height and keeping edges trim and surfaces unblemished can often be done mechanically and by not particularly experienced labour. Thus, in the more formal garden spaces around the house, maintaining proportions and a sense of space can be more or less an extension of housework – keeping the floor swept and the planting in proportion.

Richard Ayres, former head gardener at Anglesey Abbey, is among the knowledgeable volunteers prepared to put their backs into working at Marsh Lane.

Looking after apparently natural effects is far more demanding. In herbaceous and shrub borders you need to know much more about the growth habits of individual plants, and constant intervention is called for to keep the composition looking good 'artlessly'. When dealing with larger shrubs and trees, you have to combine aesthetics with a modicum of arboriculture, and think long term.

As in many different types of garden an enthusiastic bunch of volunteers contribute their time. It always says a lot about a garden that people feel strongly enough to commit themselves to its fate, but inspiring gardens often seem to make people as well as plants blossom. Volunteers play some part in almost all the gardens featured in this book. Some are active gardeners; some act as guides or stewards, helping and welcoming visitors; others tackle administration or accounts, help with fundraising and publicity, or supervise an entrance kiosk or shop. The spectrum of talents usually finds the right niche. You get retired pen-pushers cheerfully wielding chunkier tools, and ex-professionals relishing the most mundane tasks in good company and a good cause.

A streamlet with accompanying paths wanders through the Wild Garden towards the Pincey Brook. Sir Frederick planted a range of moisture-loving species along its route.

Sir Frederick Gibberd's approach was ecological, long before the term was a gardening buzzword – unlike Lawrence Johnston, who imported vast quantities of sawdust and clinker at Hidcote to allow him to create extensive areas of acid-loving planting in the alkaline Cotswold soil. By contrast, Sir Frederick planted 'with' the site, 'with nature not against it, and [using] only plants that will thrive in my garden'. He would not dream of altering the soil to suit the planting. Happily, the lower-lying areas of the Marsh Lane garden lived up to the name – there were once osier beds on the site – providing the damp soil relished by a wealth of moisture-loving plants from all over the world that make themselves at home near water. In spite of being exotics, these plants have the natural look that allows the garden margins to blend into the landscape. In contrast to the formality around the house, Sir Frederick created a Wild Garden in the valley bottom. Here there is a deliberately 'hidden garden' – a secret garden with two pools.

If he chose not to alter the natural pH of his soil, Sir Frederick didn't think twice about moving that soil around. The Pincey Brook runs along so naturally, widening into a pool of light-reflecting still water and splashing busily over a waterfall, that you would never suspect these features of being artificial. The pool was formed in 1970 by a hired digger, and the waterfall built by using bulky scrap items, including a car chassis, as caissons. Sir Frederick also moulded the little stream that runs into the pool, creating paths and bridges along

The waters of the Pincey Brook tumble innocently over the dam Sir Frederick created with a barrage of junk, recycled before the idea became hackneyed.

its length so that the varied planting of hostas, rheums, irises, flowering rushes, primulas, ferns and day-lilies could be appreciated. You don't have to be small to get lost in the labyrinth of paths here, and the gardeners' endless task is to hold back nature, clear paths and keep the area from becoming impossibly overgrown.

Views and vistas were, of course, important, such as the sightline between the gazebo and the brook. In the Wild Garden Sir Frederick discovered a good place to see the pool. It must have looked idyllically picturesque, not Modernist at all. He dubbed it the 'Kodachrome View' and graced it with one of the seats strategically placed in the lower garden. (There are areas of the garden, such as the West Vista, with no seats at all. If Sir Frederick was not a man for sitting, and expected his guests to move around the garden experiencing its spatial relationships, today's custodians might spare a thought for the more passive visiting public and place a few more welcome resting places.)

'Garden design is an art of space... The garden has become a series of rooms each with its own character, from small, intimate spaces to large, enclosed prospects.'

Sir Frederick Gibberd

You can sit quietly in a garden, even when across the valley trains hum past every few minutes, planes ply noisily overhead to and from Stansted, and 21st-century agriculture provides random mechanical accompaniments. If you are lucky, you will feel the magic of the place, and the birds that fled at your approach will return. What you will notice is the birdsong, the blossom dropping from the trees, the breezes rustling the leaves, the ever-changing light. The Gibberd Garden has naturally become a wildlife haven, as surveys of its fauna attest. Jean Farley tells with some pride that someone has found that rarity, a horse-leech – a predator of slugs – and is pleased that the un-nibbled hosta leaves are achieved through a natural balance. Chris Beardshaw is filmed finding another endangered species – a freshwater crayfish – in the Pincey Brook. The cameras also record him putting it back again. It seems that nature here is reconciled with the intrusion of Modernism.

Rheum palmatum is an ornamental rhubarb from China. Its huge leaves are overtopped in summer by tall panicles of fluffy flowers.

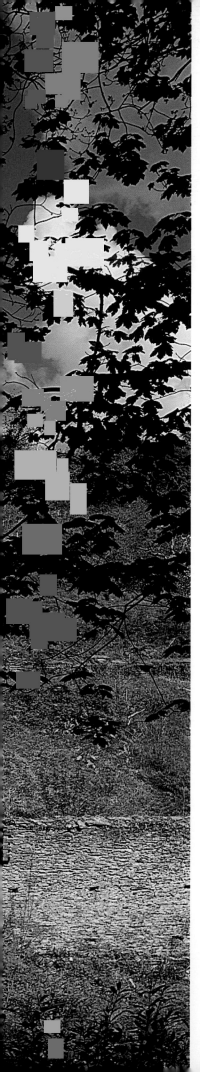

CLYNFYW
Fate of a Forgotten Kitchen Garden

Today we have supermarkets. Yesterday they had kitchen gardens, which – together with produce from the home farm and game from the estate – made country houses self-sufficient. They went to the grocer's only for exotic commodities, such as sugar, spices, tea and coffee, and to the vintner for other kinds of beverage. All over Britain there were gardens like Clynfyw's, expertly tuned to supply the entire community that depended on the 'big house' with fruit and vegetables all year round.

In a way the walled garden at Clynfyw represents a run-of-the-mill type, one of a kind you might find anywhere, like a post office or railway halt in any village. Typically, the skilled craftsmen who built it and worked in it were anonymous, everyman builders and gardeners. Their records – if any exist – lie in the shadow of their employers. It is not a case here for garden detectives of seeking the maker's motive, as at Aberglasney, or discovering it, as at Lyveden. It is not a question of period fashion, as at St Fagans, or of approaching the site via a character study of an idiosyncratic garden-maker, such as Lawrence Johnston or Sir Frederick Gibberd. At best in gardens like these you might decipher the manufacturer's stamp on some glasshouse hardware, clay pots or rusting machinery. Occasionally, someone may remember a great-grandfather, or have old photos – even, rarely, nurserymen's bills and gardeners' accounts – but such records are the icing on the cake baked from a well-tried Mrs Beeton-style Victorian receipt.

Across England a handful of kitchen gardens have recently been beautifully restored, glasshouses and all: you can see prime examples at West Dean in Sussex, Heligan in Cornwall and Audley End in Essex. They are the exceptions. In southwest Wales you might count on the fingers of one hand the walled gardens in any kind of productive cultivation.

Walled gardens turned to other uses stud the landscape, and often reveal traces of their past role. People who find themselves living and gardening on such a site may enjoy the mellow heritage of gnarled

An Outline of the Plot...

Like country-house kitchen gardens all over Britain, the 19th-century walled garden at Clynfyw on the northeastern margin of Pembrokeshire fell into neglect during the 20th century. A decline that began with manpower shortages after World War I was accelerated by 'progress' – the revolution in transport and supply that has enabled us to buy produce from shops all year round instead of growing our own according to the seasons. In areas where population is dense and land scarce, unwanted gardens make handy building plots. This can also be the case in remoter rural areas, but many sit out of sight and out of mind, quietly crumbling into dereliction.

Such was the fate of the walled garden at Clynfyw until April 2000. The seed of the idea for restoring it was a success story in the adjacent hamlet of Abercych, where the community got together to create a Millennium Garden, for which they won a Prince of Wales Award in 1999. Impressed with this growing potential, Jim Lewis-Bowen, the owner of Clynfyw, offered the 1.5-acre site to local people and organizations as a restoration project. It is now leased to the Manordeifi Community Council for 25 years at a peppercorn rent.

The Clynfyw Community Garden Group has acquired charitable status, and groups of students and volunteers have begun work to rescue the garden.

Clynfyw is near the confluence where the Cych (pronounced 'keek', with the final consonant sounded as in 'loch') joins the Teifi at Abercych. You can best locate it by looking for the point where the three counties of Pembroke, Carmarthen and Ceredigion (once Cardiganshire) touch noses. For a while they were 'lumped' (as botanists would say) together into Dyfed, but they are now 'split' again.

One small-paned glasshouse stands outside the main walls in a little hedged enclosure to the northeast. It once had a heating system to support exotic plants. A short length of old grapevine still hangs from rusting supports.

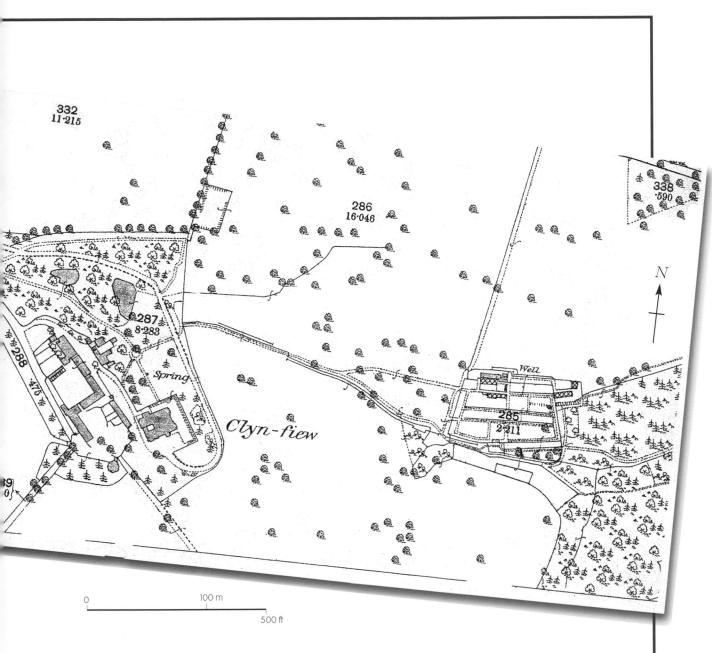

332
11·215

286
16·046

338
·590

287
8·283

288
·475

Spring

Clyn-fiew

Well

285
2·211

89
0

N

0   100 m
500 ft

The Welsh name is pronounced 'klin-view'. Variant spellings in the past include Clynview, Clyn-fiew, Clun-fyw and Clyn-fiw (the earliest, from 1684, is Klyn-view). People ask what a name means, but sometimes there's no simple translation. The element *clun* can mean a spur of land (or a human hip!) and *byw* – the verb 'to be' – signifies living, 'quick', or even virgin soil. It sounds as if someone named the site for the 'pleasantly situated' lie of the land (this happens a lot in the Welsh landscape) and for its attractive growing potential.

This section of the Ordnance Survey (OS) map of 1890 shows the house, farm and pleasure grounds (left) separated by a good 300 yards from the walled garden (right), its paths and glazed structures clearly visible.

apple trees and veteran brick-faced walls, bristling maybe with the square-hammered nails and metal ties that once supported fruit. (Garden detectives can get hooked on nails in walls, and this can lead to harder addictions, such as a fascination with greenhouse ventilation mechanisms.) There may be venerable box trees that were once knee-high edging. The soil may have a disturbingly high content of broken glass and disintegrating metal – a tetanus injection is highly recommended for all hands-on gardeners. On the 'plus' side is the fact that old walled gardens invariably offer warm, sheltered microclimates: the gardeners of the past knew just how to maximize growing potential.

Most walled kitchen gardens conform to a standard quartered design, with box-edged paths criss-crossing the garden and running around the perimeter. Thanks to geography, Clynfyw is rather different. Like most first-time visitors to this garden project, Chris Beardshaw winds his way up through the wooded valley, intent on avoiding the potholes in the twisting track for the sake of his suspension and seriously wondering if he's in the right place. If he glimpses anything to either side, it may be that the tall, drawn trees include here and there the odd exotic.

The Lie of the Land

The need to concentrate on the route evaporates with a decisive right-hand turn in the track. The suspense is over and you can at last lift your eyes upwards. Inevitably, they are drawn to an unexpected pattern on the lighter, opposite side of the valley. Supreme artifice challenges the muddled naturalism you have driven through. A rectilinear geometry is emblazoned on the sunny, south-facing slope. Suddenly the phrase 'hanging gardens' takes on meaning: this stepped garden is clinging to the steep hillside where wood gives way to farmland. It's apparently in isolation, with no buildings to be seen.

On closer focus you realize the geometry is blurred. The walls are crumbling, the paths and terraces not clearly defined. This is a garden in need of tender loving care. Closer still, it becomes evident that something is happening. There are signs of human activity.

The Walled Garden from the west, showing its steep south-facing slope. The Gothic Gateway is further uphill to the left.

One of the espaliered apple trees, still fruiting but as yet unidentified. No longer severely trained along wires, it has thrown out branches in all directions and keeled off its position atop one of the terrace walls.

People can fall in love with gardens like this. Indeed, people can fall in love *in* gardens like this. Tina Sacco from Cardigan, who leads the community project, used to come to the overgrown Eden of Clynfyw in her courting days. In country districts it's an innocent-enough pastime of a summer's evening to go poking about old deserted buildings and their gardens as Tina did. On one tryst her lover reached out to pick her the very juiciest of the apples from a nearby tree. He toppled over and disappeared for some moments into the undergrowth. (He had literally come across one of the hidden terraces.) When he emerged with an abashed expression – and the prize apple to offer his beloved – Tina was won over. 'If he was prepared to do that, he was the man for me!' They now have a family, and Tina chairs the committee planning the future of Clynfyw's kitchen garden. A local grapevine operates to generate interest and bring volunteers to help in the garden. People living in cottages once occupied by sawyers, clog-makers and wood turners, farm labourers and quarrymen are invited to participate in the therapeutic activity of gardening together in a good cause.

The Tivyside Heyday

In the old world of the Anglicized squirearchy the Teifi valley had a relatively high density of gentry estates, particularly as the river approached the seaport of Cardigan. It was known as 'Tivyside', and its prosperity in the context of the late 18th and the 19th centuries was the equivalent of today's 'M4 corridor' in south Wales – a flourishing artery penetrating into difficult terrain. Today the Teifi valley seems remote. Its economy depends on the tourist attraction of a pretty river just large enough to make canoeing exciting, and on farmers urged to survive by diversifying. In the mid-19th century, however, the river was a lively waterway and its valley was studded with modest industrial sites and the homes of prosperous landowners. John Nash (1752–1835), architect of Brighton Pavilion and other landmarks, cut his teeth designing some of them. Upstream there was a lively woollen industry. Downstream there was slate quarrying. Locally there were pockets of activity, including iron-working, the occupation by which early owners of Clynfyw gained their wealth.

'The vicinity is ornamented with several gentlemen's seats,' wrote Samuel Lewis in his *Topographical Dictionary* (1834) of the parish of Manerdivy (as Manordeifi was then known). He mentioned the prestigious neighbouring properties of Pentre and Ffynone, and added that 'Clynview, the seat of T. Lewis, Esq., is also a handsome residence pleasingly situated, and embellished with scenery of interesting character'. The 'handsome residence' was not pleasing enough by 1850. To celebrate his marriage, William Henry Lewis built a fashionable new house for his bride Mary Colby of nearby Rhosygilwen, sister to John Colby of Ffynone (house by Nash). We presume that the new kitchen-garden complex sited some quarter-mile from the new house was built at about the same time.

The Victorians knew just what they were up to when it came to kitchen gardens. Aside from all the technological expertise involved in defying winter cold with frames and glasshouses, they could size up the best spot available for outdoor gardening. At Clynfyw the chosen aspect for the new kitchen garden faced due south, where the steep gradient could optimize the growing potential of the sun's warmth. The climate in sheltered westerly Wales has none of Cornwall's mildness – this is cold gardening country. At least there was an ample

Traditionally, in kitchen gardens, stone walls were faced with brick on the sunny side. Bricks absorbed and retained the sun's warmth, helping fruit to ripen on trees trained against them. With the capping stones dislodged, roots and weather can penetrate a wall. Here the brick lining is peeling away like wallpaper.

supply of water, for power as well as irrigation. The generator installed in 1908 (embossed Gilkes & Co Kendall) is still there. Terracing the sloping site must have been an expensive exercise, as must constructing the walls (the south-facing ones lined with heat-retaining bricks, stamped 'Woodward & Co./Cardigan'). The heated glasshouse ranges situated towards the top of the garden would have been chosen from manufacturers' catalogues.

Project manager Robert Taylor is no Victorian, but his years of experience in hands-on horticulture – he started in the days of the five-year apprenticeship – make him virtually a gardener of the old school, and a particularly informative teacher and leader. At Clynfyw his disciples include college students, local volunteers, parties from youth organizations, disabled groups and even young offenders.

Robert Taylor is fascinating to listen to as he explains how a garden like this was carefully planned with its walls angled to maximize the available sunlight, and to allow frost to roll away downhill without damaging plants. Walls and shelter gave the Victorian gardener precise control over the timing of crops. Outdoors as well as under glass, every inch of ground was used. Sunny and shady aspects of walls, warmer and cooler levels of ground were all taken into account, for it was not only a question of coaxing early crops with extra warmth and forcing techniques, but prolonging the seasons so that the succession of summer vegetables and fruit did not peak too soon. There was a whole household of servants to feed, as well as the family and its visitors.

But before anyone can do much orthodox gardening here the site has to be cleared and interpreted. When the rescue project started, the four stepped terraces were masked in vegetation. Overgrown espaliers had collapsed, providing extra frameworks for the fabric of brambles and knotweed to weave shapeless webs over them. Two or three generations of disuse not only make a devilish mess of a once well-tended plot; they also obliterate the memories that might help today's keen new minds.

Details on OS maps help today's restorers to identify hidden features. Sometimes there's an explicit piece of evidence, commemorating a date – a plaque set in the topmost wall records that this section of the garden was enlarged in 1925–6. (Perhaps it was then that some of the older glasshouses were superseded by angled-steel structures, with panes attached to horizontal rods by patent metal clips.) Then there's the serendipity of family records. In a perfect world old houses have their gardens extensively documented in well-captioned photograph albums. A while after the restoration project got under way at Clynfyw, Tom Lewis-Bowen, Jim's father, found some inscrutable negatives safely preserved in an old tin. The BBC team arranged for these to be developed, and two of them turned out to be views of the walled garden taken around 1910.

Opposite Broken terracotta forcing pots gather moss in the corner Robert Taylor has dubbed the 'elephants' graveyard', while Chris Beardshaw examines an interesting piece of horticultural salvage – the patent 'Pluviette Sprinkler'.

Below A slate plaque in the upper wall tells that the garden was extended in 1925–6 by 'RLB' – Ruth Lewis-Bowen. How useful it would be for garden restorers if more people had made such records!

Pictures in the Attic

The first of the newly discovered photographs (right) shows the Gothic Gateway leading into the garden. Sunlight falls squarely on the west-facing wall. The brim-shaded faces suggest a garden of a golden afternoon in spring. The younger boys wear guernseys and keep watch over a jampot – for minnows or frogspawn collected from the nearby pool? The Sealyham terrier (a Pembrokeshire breed) studies the faintly enquiring tilt in the stance of Mrs Lewis-Bowen. Her husband has a generous flower in his buttonhole – something from a greenhouse. It's the size of the jampot top. It must be a deep colour to be this dark in the photograph.

The Gothic Gateway is the posh way into the Walled Garden, more ceremonial than the other entrances. Its archway is outlined in sawn slate, matching the coping along the top of the wall (each coping stone rebated to overlap its neighbour and dispatch rain-water down the slope). It stands at the end of the main pathway from the house, a route for pedestrians. There must have been another route for workaday exchanges: barrowloads of fruit and vegetables towards the house, cartloads of steaming muck from the farmyard near by.

The doorway reveals a glimpse of the glasshouse with an ornate finial that Robert Taylor thinks may have been the pine-house – its paintwork beautifully gleaming. The path is smooth and swept clean, and the fragment of edging we can see below Mrs Lewis-Bowen's left hand on the door handle looks like dwarf box. The distant background behind her head is a muddy glimpse of trees. But what's this filling the top of the arch? It looks like some broad overhead framework with branches trained over it. A rose arch or arbour, perhaps, just inside the garden. Long gone.

The Gothic Gateway today, with a makeshift wicket gate. (The original pointed door stands inside the garden.)

The boys in the photo sit and stand on steps ascending the slope. Nothing is grown against this wall. Today this area is overgrown with trees. (You can see their shadows on the wall, opposite.) The steps near the wall have disappeared and in their place we find a mystery. A planting bed has been created against the wall sometime in the intervening years. The recycled slate edging to the bed is the curiosity. It's made of slabs the size of a coffee table, each punctuated at regular intervals by holes about an inch in diameter. They look like some kind of slate grille (this is slate country). What and where was their original function?

Thomas Edward and Ruth Lewis-Bowen stand at the Gothic Gateway, their children and Sealyham terrier alongside them. James William (grandfather of Jim) leans against the wall, his younger siblings Gerald and Edward (often taken as twins) sitting on the steps. The friend in the white hat is unknown.

The Lewis-Bowen boys on the terrace are (from left to right) James William and, with an unidentified friend between them, the younger brothers, Edward and Gerald. Their father faces us on the path. The young lady on the right could be his eldest child, Dorothea.

The photo of the Espalier Walk (above) takes us inside the garden, on the next cross-path down the hill. The same four lads are deployed on the left-hand, uphill terrace wall. It's not such a sunny day, and hats are not required. Father (it looks like the same cap) is in more workaday attire. The Sealyham has obeyed the order to 'Sit!' Two ladies of the family (never hatless outdoors) pose on the path. Further off in the vegetable bed to the right an anonymous weederwoman is caught in action, back bent over the hoe.

We see espaliered apples trained on wires on top of the wall, and against the face of the wall itself, laden with blossom. A narrow line of bulb leaves runs along the foot of the wall. The right-hand, downhill side of the path has dwarf box edging.

Today you can find traces of the terrace wall but this path is hidden under a gradient of soil that runs continuously into the slope of the garden. Most of the apple trees have disappeared altogether, but near the centre of the garden one or two, as if to compensate, have grown to gigantic proportions and collapsed under their own weight. Robert Taylor scrutinizes this photograph with delight. One thing that has survived *in situ* is the occasional iron stanchion from the espalier supports. With the aid of a bit of geometry it should be possible to work out the width of the path. Another step forward. Will any of the box edging still be found along this path, as it has down the eastern side of the garden? Unlikely: you would know if it had. The stumps of the box edging there are a handspan across. We hope whoever cut them down appreciated their worth. Boxwood is one of the classics for wood engravers.

The state of one of the two cross-paths in early spring 2002, before clearance. An attempt has been made to define the width with staked timbers.

There are other ways of making discoveries. Enter the North Pembrokeshire Metal Detectors' Group. Along with a couple of old pennies and some miscellaneous loops and buckles, the most exciting finds were fruit-tree labels. Several were apples, but there were two pears.

A label that was read at first as 'Carn's Pippin' did not appear in the reference books. A closer look at the damaged first letters came up with the name 'Fearn's Pippin' – a brilliant scarlet apple raised in Fulham before 1780, prized for the dining table and reputed to be among the Victorian top-dozen varieties. Another great apple of that era is 'Bismarck', from the 1850s. This tallies with the date of the making of the garden. The espaliered apple trees hand-to-hand along the terraces would have been an intrinsic part of the garden plan. Pears are different. There's a group of trees originally trained as cordons against the 'new' 1920s' section of wall in the northwest corner of the garden. These might be newer varieties.

It only remains to match the labels with the remaining trees. Autumnal Apple Days have become a popular feature of the gardening

The displaced fruit-tree labels found by the metal detectors are prime clues – like fingerprints – in the garden detectives' quest, and these machine-made products may be datable. But they still need to be matched with their host trees, if any still exist.

calendar. You should correlate blossom and leaf as well as fruit for a full identification, but the shape, size, coloration and skin texture – plus the detailed characteristics of crown (where the petals were attached) and the stem attachment – can be sufficient, especially when you have a running start by knowing what some of the names might be.

Without yearly pruning these trees have run riot over the last 50 years. The 1910 photographs on the previous pages show the 'before' state of the espaliered trees on the terrace. The characteristic parallel side branches have mostly died out, the plant's vigour heading skywards. Trees planted on top of a terrace wall have only half the normal 360-degree root run, so when they become top-heavy are doubly likely to keel over downhill. This may not stop them growing, so more branches grow upwards, distorting the pattern beyond recognition. Without the garden context, you could easily be unaware that they had ever been grown as espaliers. (Yet they may fruit as well as ever.)

Tackling seriously overgrown trained fruit trees presents a dilemma. Normally it's a good idea to start by cutting out wood that is obviously dead, and an eager but ignorant restorer might well do so. However,

Fruit Tree Labels at Clynfyw

Northern Spy

Allington Pippin: Late cooker/ dessert apple from Lincolnshire, before 1884.
Bismarck: Tasmanian late cooking apple, 1850s.
Bramley's Seedling: Late cooker raised in Nottingham-shire in early 1800s. Widely planted from 1880s.
Court of Wick: Late dessert apple, 1790, also known as Wood's Huntingdon.
Easterbeurre: French pear, also known as Doyenne d'Hiver.

Fearn's Pippin: English dessert apple, 1780s.
Gooseberry Apple: Kentish late cooking apple, 1830s.
Lane's Prince Albert: Late cooker from Hertfordshire, pre-1841.
Mother: American apple, 1820s. The 19th-century pomologist Robert Hogg described it as having a 'balsamatic aroma'.
Northern Spy: American late dessert apple, 1800.
Reinette du Canada: French dessert apple, 1770s.

Opposite, top Volunteers building supports along the terraces for a new set of espaliered apple trees.

Opposite, bottom Unidentified raspberry canes rescued from the wilderness are being replanted in cleared soil to see how they bear.

those outstretched arms, albeit withered, are the signposts that show that trees were once espaliers, and since their gnarled profiles tell the story of years of close pruning, it is worth leaving them be. Robert Taylor marks the wood that is to be pruned away in early spring, before the sap rises, starting with the most wayward branches whose weight could unbalance or break the whole plant. The students and volunteers help with the sawing. Over a period of several years he plans to bring the trees more or less back into line. As spring begins, he demonstrates a variety of grafting techniques on the spot, and his students learn that it may be feasible to use grafts to restore something of the lost shapes. No synthetics here: he ties his new grafts in place with raffia and protects them from the elements with a satisfyingly plastic mix of two parts clay to one part cow dung (to retain moisture). The ghosts of past gardeners nod their approval.

New fruit trees are coming in, too; replacements, that is – not novelties. Besides a few of the original apples recorded on the labels, a selection of trees typical of a Victorian garden are being introduced. The supplier is Paul Davis, whose nursery specializes in old varieties. The benefit may work two ways. Paul Davis is hoping that pear 'Easterbeurre' is still extant in the garden: he would dearly like to get some grafting material from it. The same goes for the rare 'Gooseberry Apple'. Clynfyw may turn out to have 'heritage fruit value'.

To support the young trees volunteers re-create the espalier supports along the terrace walls. They use wooden posts and wires this time. Pierced iron stanchions and patent wire stretchers as used in the old days will have to wait for a more prosperous phase of restoration.

Organic Partners

The home farm at Clynfyw proudly attained organic status in 2001. Although the walled garden is strictly a separate enterprise from the estate proper, the project undertook to respect the ethos of the surroundings and to operate along organic lines. 'A rod for your own backs,' someone comments. And wouldn't it be easier to zap that sea of rampant vegetation with glyphosate? Perhaps you have to be an optimist to be a gardener, but Robert Taylor doesn't want to risk losing an accumulation of beneficial garden wildlife, and perhaps some

precious old plants, along with the weeds. (There's always the seed of a chance that something old and rare might be found, or a new hybrid. One day we might all want to grow the 'Clynfyw' gooseberry, or daffodil, or apple.) So it's softly, softly to see what's there, and on with the mulch. Among the early expenditures were rolls of Geotex sheeting, a membrane that suppresses weed germination by excluding light. You lay it over areas dug ready for planting and along paths before adding your chosen topping of gravel or woodchips. Another of Robert Taylor's tactics is to strim, then mow, and keep mowing. In theory, in

time, broad-leaved weeds surrender to the determined mower. Only grass renews itself from the base to survive repeated assaults on its leaves. (Try telling that to creeping buttercups.)

One of the biggest national assets in the organic mission is the Henry Doubleday Research Association (HDRA) of Ryton Organic Gardens near Coventry. The Victorian kitchen garden at Audley End in Essex has recently been restored and is being run along organic principles in partnership with the HDRA. Chris Beardshaw finds that a visit to Audley End makes a telling comparison with Clynfyw, although the two gardens are poles apart. Audley End sits comfortably on level ground, in pristine condition, part of a large estate in a wealthy and populous part of the Home Counties, with full-time staff (never enough of them, of course) and plenty of visitors queuing to buy its produce. Some 200 miles due west, steeply sloping Clynfyw is in serious decay, at the back of beyond, with just a handful of volunteers

Authenticity extends to the way seeds are stored and transported. No steamy plastic bags here, but screw-top glass jars and paper envelopes.

Robert Taylor, officially project manager, contemplating the activities of his students and helpers. The derelict glasshouse in the background is the one glimpsed in the old photograph on page 155.

broaching the immense task of rescue. And yet there's a mass of practical information to be gained, as well as a bright gleam of inspiration.

If Audley End represents an ideal, the perfect picture on the lid of a jigsaw-puzzle box, it can help to identify and place in context some of the incomplete fragments found at Clynfyw. Literal examples come from that 'elephants' graveyard' in a corner of the upper garden, where lumbering terracotta shapes, none of them whole, lie heaped up and gathering moss, a memorial to a lost gardening tradition. Go to Audley End and you can see an armoury of these blanching and forcing pots put to use in the cultivation of forgotten vegetables, such as seakale, as well as the more familiar rhubarb and chicory. There you also find a fine range of fruit trees trained along wires and against walls in a variety of traditional patterns, some of which must have been applied at Clynfyw. Best of all is the suite of restored glasshouses and frames, each expertly designed for a specific use, for the apricots, grapes, cucumbers and melons that we now buy from supermarket shelves, or for tender exotic flowers to show off to friends and visitors. Deciphering the glasshouse code is a branch of garden history all of its own.

What to cultivate at Clynfyw? Why not take an adventurous approach from the very start? As more ground is cleared and crop production becomes a serious business with regular customers to satisfy, some off-the-peg modern varieties may be grown. Meanwhile, why not experiment with 'heritage' plants no longer available commercially? Grow unusual vegetables not just as curiosities (although old varieties can be a positive attraction for gardening visitors) but to make a valuable contribution to horticulture, by monitoring their progress in a new environment and (it is hoped) replenishing the seed bank.

To Audley End again, where head gardener Michael Thurlow supplies some vegetable seed and a box of cabbage and pea seedlings for Clynfyw. The varieties are largely 19th century, obtainable now only from the Heritage Seed Library. They include the Victorian onion 'Up to Date', a white beetroot called 'White Devoy' and the crimson-flowered broad bean that is one of the HDRA's flagship varieties. The old variety of pea named 'Ne Plus Ultra' tells its own tale. It was almost lost to cultivation when someone found a handful in an old gardener's pocket and planted them. It's not just old gardens that need rescuing, but plants, too.

Gardens for People

I came to Clynfyw on a sunny April morning when no one else was here. Hoverflies and several kinds of bee vouchsafed Robert Taylor's faith in the presence of beneficial wildlife, and two lady-birds were energetically ensuring the presence of future ladybirds.

'Gardens are for growing people as well as plants.'

Charles Stirton

Armed with canes and labels, I intended to mark some of the clumps of daffodils I had managed to get identified – including the old double 'Van Sion' – before the flowers disappeared. In the fortnight since I had collected the specimens the undergrowth had switched to fast-forward mode and brambles were establishing their devilish geodesic structure at human thigh height. With secateurs, I was snipping a narrow path through to a distant *Narcissus pseudonarcissus* cultivar when something below the bramble dome caught my eye. A pattern of brown on

On 2 May 2002 the wider community came to Clynfyw – to contribute, not just to view.

Above Paths take shape and the framework for training new espaliers is put in place on top of cleared terrace walls.

Opposite Old gardens inspire enthusiasm: you can work in a team or as an individual. Whether you know your onions, seek solace in therapeutic weeding, or have excess energy to expend, the boss can point you in the right direction. It's vocational. It's a learning process, and a rewarding one.

brown. A rounded shape with the kind of stillness that can only be alive. Stooping to see better, I found myself eye to eye with a hen pheasant, brave and motionless on her nest.

Again I felt like a trespasser. With apologies for my intrusion, I skirted her domain and positioned the last label as respectfully as I could. She never moved. I crept away to a cleared path and sat on a step soaking up the welcome sun and thinking what to write about.

The next time I came the whole walled garden seemed alive. A kind of joyous jungle-bashing jamboree had been organized for 2 May 2002. Local gardening societies, members of the Hardy Plant Society, anyone in the area with a gardening bent was invited to join the regulars to lend a hand and make a difference, largely in a specified area between the two main cross-axes and the central uphill path. (Mrs Pheasant and her nest below the main wall were undisturbed.)

The sun shone. Weeds were weeded. Vegetables were planted. Cadets wheeled barrowloads of gravel, Geotex was unrolled and paths appeared. Posts were sunk and strung with wires. Strangers worked and sweated together and as they talked found common ground and became friends.

A part of the garden was growing goodness again.

Not quite the traditional bird's-eye view, but from across the valley the tiered human figures give scale to the layered terraces, almost like a cartoon-strip story. Imagine what a picture a Bruegel might make of this jamboree-day activity, or in what splendid stylized images the Egyptian tomb-painters might depict the concentration with which the volunteer gardeners work. Watch this space – or come and join in.

Sources & References

Lyveden New Bield

Lyveden New Bield and the Tresham family have been well documented over centuries. The excellent National Trust Guidebook *Lyveden New Bield* by Mark Girouard (1990) includes a bibliography summarizing the principal historical sources.

Additional detail on the family and finances of Sir Thomas Tresham can be found in M.E. Finch, *The Wealth of Five Northamptonshire Families*, Northamptonshire Record Society, Vol. xix (1956).

Enticing illustrated articles include Mark Girouard's 'Still Waters, Still Deep', in *Country Life* (11 February 1993), and Stephen Anderton's 'Passion Plays' in *The Garden*, Vol. 125, Part 1 (January 2000).

The most exhaustive recent documentation is the work of Clare Bense, *The Elizabethan Water Garden at Lyveden*, Research Undertaken for the National Trust (unpublished, 1998).

Other information in this chapter comes from notes by and personal communication with Mark Bradshaw, Curator.

The complex background to gardens of the period is brilliantly illuminated by Roy Strong in *The Renaissance Garden in England* (1979, revised 1998) and *The Artist and the Garden* (2000).

The Brogdale Horticultural Trust has been helpful with information on old varieties of fruit. For an excellent account specifically of apples, Joan Morgan and Alison Richards's *The Book of Apples* (1993), published in association with Brogdale, is recommended.

Aberglasney

The principal summary of the history of Aberglasney is currently the author's own *A Garden Lost in Time* (1999), which includes an extensive list of sources. The book was reviewed in the Welsh Historic Gardens Trust's *Bulletin* (Summer 1999) by Caroline Palmer, who used the review to advance her useful theory that garden history is a branch of anthropology.

The two seminal sources specified in the present text are the article by Francis Jones, 'Aberglasney and Its Families' in *National Library of Wales Journal*, Vol. XXI (1979) and M.A.Rudd, *Records of the Rudd Family* (1920).

The poetry of Aberglasney is celebrated in Gillian Clarke's *Nine Green Gardens* (2000).

For a full summary of the excavations by Cambrian Archaeological Projects, see Kevin Blockley, *Aberglasney House and Garden: Archaeology, History and Architecture*, British Archaeological Report – British Series 334 (2002).

The archives and personnel of Aberglasney Restoration Trust are, as ever, a repository of both useful information and further occasions for puzzlement!

Also relevant to Aberglasney's early history are the two titles by Roy Strong cited under Lyveden.

St Fagans

The Museum of Welsh Life is furnished with splendid archives peopled by informative and dedicated staff. Among the key documents they produced are:

Hugh Pettigrew, *Handlist of Roses* (privately printed 1904).

Christine Stevens, 'The St Fagans Portion of the Plymouth Estate c.1850– c.1950', MPhil Thesis, University of Swansea (1998).

Anon. [H. Avray Tipping], 'St Fagans Castle, Cardiff' in *Country Life* (20 September 1902).

Walburga, Lady Paget, *In My Tower* (1924).

Two recently published articles that were as informative as their authors have been helpful are Andrew Dixey, 'A Rosary Revived' in *The Rose* (Christmas 1998) and Deborah Evans, 'The Gardens of the Earls of Plymouth at St Fagans Castle, Cardiff', in *Gerddi*, the Journal of the Welsh Historic Gardens Trust, Vol. III (2000/2001).

For a general introduction to St Fagans, see Eurwyn William, *St Fagans Castle and Its Inhabitants* (1988), and for background information on Gay Windsor and her set, consult Jane Abdy & Charlotte Gere, *The Souls* (1984).

Opposite The Knot Garden at St Fagans.

Hidcote

Like Lyveden, Hidcote has been exhaustively written about. Again, a first-class National Trust guidebook, Anna Pavord's *Hidcote Manor Garden* (National Trust, 1993) makes an excellent introduction to the garden, and provides a good summary of the principal published sources. For a more leisurely read, consult Ethne Clarke, *Hidcote: The Making of a Garden* (1989). (Both include quotations from commentators such as James Lees-Milne, Nancy and Norah Lindsay and Vita Sackville-West.)

Invaluable both for its formidable compilation of up-to-date information and for its inclusion of extensive articles, notes and correspondence (some unpublished) is National Trust historian Katie Fretwell's *Hidcote Manor Garden Survey 1999–2000* (2000). This includes Forrest's letter and a draft article by Nancy Lindsay among other fascinating material.

Other very helpful information derives from personal communication with the head gardener, Glyn Jones.

The Gibberd Garden

The author's first encounter with the Marsh Lane Garden came on reading 'Princeling's Pleasure', an article by Jane Brown in *Gardens Illustrated* (October/November 1995). Enormously useful on matters of detail is the report prepared by Land Use Consultants, *The Gibberd Garden: Landscape Survey and Restoration Management Plan* (October 1997).

A novel source of material came in the form of the video of the BBC *Omnibus* programme of 12 December 1982 – a most illuminating glimpse into the hidden past.

Individual members of the Gibberd Gardens Trust, volunteers and gardeners provided helpful information, and Lady Patricia Gibberd's thoughtful comments were particularly welcome.

Clynfyw

Here the research is only just beginning. Outline information on Clynfyw compiled by C.S. Briggs is recorded on the RCAHMW [Royal Commission of Ancient and Historical Monuments Wales] Extended National Database, which includes a splendidly thorough description of the Walled Garden by Gerry Hudson of the Welsh Historic Gardens Trust (July 2001).

For background reading and historical context Francis Jones, *Historic Houses of Pembrokeshire* (1996) and Leslie Baker-Jones, *Princelings, Privilege and Power: the Tivyside Gentry in Their Community* (1999) both help to set the scene. Some of the sources cited in their bibliographies might be worth further exploration.

See also B.G. Charles, *Placenames of Pembrokeshire*, 2 vols, (1992).

The quotation by Charles Stirton comes from a speech made when, as Director of the National Botanic Garden of Wales, he was publicizing this forthcoming attraction.

Readers of Welsh might be interested in Clynfyw's incidental appearance in a local murder story: Gwylon Phillips, *Llofruddiaeth Shadrach Lewis* (1986).

For anyone interested in the history of productive gardens, Susan Campbell's *Charleston Kedding: A History of Kitchen Gardening* (1996) is essential reading.

Clynfyw Community Garden Trust furnished useful documentation, John Savidge assisted with daffodil identification, Jim Lewis-Bowen was helpful and enthusiastic on family matters, and Robert Taylor has an endless wealth of fascinating knowledge on old gardens and present-day gardening.

Index

Illustrations are indicated by *italic* type.

Acknowledgements

It's always a treat to have an excuse to visit gardens and meet gardeners, and especially to go behind the scenes and see the hidden bits. I am grateful to the powers that be in the various organizations responsible for the different gardens – the National Trust, the Aberglasney Restoration Trust, the Museum of Welsh Life, the Gibberd Garden Trust and the Clynfyw Community Garden Group – for allowing an enquiring author and a persistent photographer such free access to their gardens. Our failure to find old roses flowering and old apples fruiting in February was not their fault.

The BBC Cymru Wales team has shared a wealth of research material, theories and therapies, and has been fun to work with. Very special thanks to John Trefor for his inspiring help, and to his team – Lynda, Shreepali, Catrin, Sally, Ros, Rob and Martin – as well as to the star of the show, Chris Beardshaw.

It's impossible to mention all the individual gardeners, volunteers and friends who have helped in different ways. Special thanks to Richard Ayres, Mark Bradshaw, Gillian Clarke, Elwyn Couser, Andrew Dixey, Jennette Emery-Wallis, Deborah Evans, Jean Farley, Katie Fretwell, Lady Patricia Gibberd, Craig Hamilton, Gerry Hudson, Lowri Hughes, Glyn Jones, Jim Lewis-Bowen, Tom Lloyd, Gerallt Nash, Jane Quinton, Graham Rankin, John Savidge, Christine Stevens, Robert Taylor and Alan Wilson.

Enormous thanks to a very special book 'team' – editor Trish Burgess and designer Judith Robertson – hustled and organized by Pippa Rubinstein and Robin Douglas-Withers. Rowan Isaac is as lovely to work with as his photographs are to look at. I'd collaborate with any of them again at the drop of a hat.

In spite of all this excellent advice and attention, the opinions expressed in the book are those of the author alone.

Picture Credits

All pictures by Rowan Isaac, apart from the following. Page 13, Garden plan by Robin Griggs (RHS) and *The Garden* magazine; 14, Kate Attwooll; 16, By kind permission of His Grace the Duke of Buccleugh and Queensberry, KT; 21, 27, By permission of the British Library (MS Add 39831 Folio 3) and (MS 39828-39838 Tresham Papers); 40–1, Garden plan and section by Michael Ibbotson from garden designs by Colvin & Moggridge (Landscape Consultants to the Aberglasney Restoration Trust); 53, 56, Craig Hamilton; 57, Courtesy of Camarthen Record Office; 58, Private collection; 59, Kathy de Witt; 68–9, National Museum and Galleries of Wales; 70, Private collection; 71, By kind permission of the Earl of Plymouth; 76, 77, National Museum and Galleries of Wales; 78, Peter Beales; 84, 85, National Museum and Galleries of Wales; 94–5, Garden plan by permission of the National Trust; 100, Anthony Denny © House & Garden/Condé Nast Publications Ltd; 121, Garden plan by Jennette Emery-Wallis; 129, 130, By permission of the Gibberd Archive; 146–7, Mapping reproduced with permission from the Ordnance Survey, who can provide copies of the original mapping from their vast archive. For more information visit www.ordnance survey.co.uk; 155, 156, By kind permission of the Lewis-Bowen family.

While every effort has been made to trace present copyright holders, the publisher apologizes in advance for any unintentional error or omission, and will be pleased to insert the appropriate acknowledgement in any subsequent edition.

Gazeteer

All details correct at time of going to press.

CLYNFYW

Clynfyw Countryside Centre
Abercych
Boncath
Pembrokeshire SA37 0HF

Telephone: 01239 682209
(Chairperson, Community
Garden Group)
01239 682190 (Sec)

E-mail: Eifion.abercych@talk21.com

Website: www.clynfyw.co.uk

Admission: Free

Open: By arrangement. Please
telephone for information.

ABERGLASNEY

Aberglasney Restoration Trust
Llangathen
Carmarthenshire SA32 8QH

Telephone: 01558 668998

E-mail: info@aberglasney.org

Website: www.aberglasney.org

Directions: On A40, 4 miles west
of Llandeilo. Turn south at
Broadoak crossroads.

Admission: Adults £5;
Pensioners £4,
Children & disabled £2.50;
Family £12. Group discounts
available.

Open: Daily 10 a.m. – 6 p.m.;
winter 10.30 a.m. – 4 p.m.

LYVEDEN NEW BIELD

(National Trust)

Nr Oundle
Peterborough
Northants PE8 5AT

Telephone: 01832 205358

E-mail:
Lyvedennewbield@ntrust.org.uk

Website: www.nationaltrust.org.uk

Directions: 4 miles southwest of
Oundle via A427.

Admission: £2;
parties by arrangement.

Open: Daily except Mon & Tues
(open bank holidays),
Apr – Oct , 10 .30 a.m. – 5 p.m.
Sat & Sun, Nov – Mar, 10 .30 a.m.
– 4 p.m.

ST FAGANS

Museum of Welsh Life
St Fagans
Cardiff CF5 6XB

Telephone: 02920 573500

E-mail: mwl@ngmw.ac.uk

Website: www.nmgw.ac.uk

Directions: Signposted from
junction 44 of M4. Direct access
from A4232.

Admission: Free

Open: Daily 10 .00 a.m. – 5 p.m.

HIDCOTE (National Trust)

Hidcote Bartrim
nr Chipping Campden
Glos GL55 6LR

Telephone: 01386 438333
(infoline 01684 855370)

E-mail: Hidcote@ntrust.org.uk

Website:
www.nationaltrust.org.uk
/hidcote

Directions: 4 miles northeast
of Chipping Campden, 1 mile
east of B4632, off B4081.

Admission: Individual £5.80;
Family £14.50

Open: Mar – Nov, 11 a.m. – 5.30
p.m.; Nov – Dec, Fri, Sat,
Sun 12 – 4 p.m.

THE GIBBERD GARDEN

The Gibberd Garden Trust
The Barn
Marsh Lane
Gilden Way
Harlow
Essex CM17 0NA

Telephone: 01279 442112

Website:
www.thegibberdgarden.co.uk

Directions: Signposted off the
B183 Harlow – Hatfield Heath
Road.

Admission: Adults £3;
Concessions £2;
Accompanied children free.

Open: Apr – Oct, Sat, Sun
& bank holidays, 2–6 p.m.
Group bookings on weekdays
by arrangement.

Cardigan

CLYNFYW

Carmarthen

Swansea

ST FAGANS

Cardiff

ABERGLASNEY

Bristol

Worcester

Northampton

HIDCOTE

Oxford

London

Harlow

Peterborough

LYVEDEN NEW BIELD

Cambridge

THE GIBBERD GARD